PASQUAL

Born in Nebraska, Michael Rips practices criminal law in New York. He is married to the artist Sheila Berger, and he lives at the Chelsea Hotel in Manhattan.

Michael Rips

PASQUALE'S NOSE

Adventures in a Small Town in Italy

VINTAGE

Published by Vintage 2002

2 4 6 8 10 9 7 5 3 1

Book design by Chicka Azuma.
Illustrations by Rodica Prato

First published in Great Britain in 2001 by
Chatto & Windus

Vintage
Random House, 20 Vauxhall Bridge Road,
London SW1V 2SA

Random House Australia (Pty) Limited
20 Alfred Street, Milsons Point, Sydney,
New South Wales 2061, Australia

Random House New Zealand Limited
18 Poland Road, Glenfield, Auckland 10,
New Zealand

Random House (Pty) Limited
Endulini, 5A Jubilee Road, Parktown 2193,
South Africa

The Random House Group Limited Reg. No. 954009
www.randomhouse.co.uk

A CIP catalogue record for this book
is available from the British Library

ISBN 0 09 942273 5

Papers used by Random House are natural, recyclable products made from wood grown in sustainable forests. The manufacturing processes conform to the environmental regulations of the country of origin

Printed and bound in Great Britain by
Cox & Wyman Ltd, Reading, Berkshire

for Sheila and Nicolaïa

Contents

Contents

A C K N O W L E D G M E N T S
For their contributions to this book I would like to thank
Esther Allen, Kurt Andersen, Nicole Aragi, Judy Clain,
Jill Connelly, Sarah Crichton, Romolo De Marchis,
Luciano De Marco, Paolo Gnecco, Michael Gorchov, the
Guidis, Romain Lamaze, Christina Odone, Joe O'Neill,
Harlan Rips, Claudio di Simone, and Michele Zalopany.

N

Via di Ronciglione

Piazza Cavour

Piazza del Comun

Convento di S. Paolo

SUTRI

S. Maria Assunta

Chiesa di S. Maria del Parto

Via Cassia

Villa Savorelli

Anfiteatro

Chiesa di S. Maria del Monte

Roma →

Necropoli Rupestre

Pasquale's Nose

FOR as long as I can remember I have suffered from the belief that the place where I am living, however wretched, is preferable to anywhere else, however pleasant—the brown grass here is better than the green grass there.

My brown grass that spring was the Riss Restaurant, a purgatorial place where I would sit day after day doing little or nothing, surrounded by others doing less. It was at the Riss that Sheila found me, at the Riss that she suggested that we move to Italy, and at the Riss that I refused to go.

Sheila, an artist, had just given birth to our child. With no reason to believe that I would ever work, she felt compelled to earn money. That's where Italy came in.

Sheila knew of a medieval town at the top of a hill in central Italy. Artists lived there and one of them had a vacant house and studio. The town and studio would inspire her to complete a new series of paintings, which she would sell to support us. As for me, Sheila claimed that the town had two or three coffee shops that were as awful as the Riss.

I began to assemble the excuses for not going. But Sheila didn't need to hear them—she knew them from countless other conversations, all of which ended the same way: I would not leave.

But that afternoon something happened. A sheet of paper taped to the cash register. A sign.

The Riss, which had been open twenty-four hours a day, seven days a week, for seven decades, was closing.

It should not have surprised me—unlike Heaven and Hell, Purgatory was bound by time, subject to decay and oblivion.

Days later we left for Italy.

That Sheila was responsible for the sign on the cash register did not occur to me until it was too late.

The Guidi

UPON arriving in Sutri, I made my way to the central square and found three cafés.

I chose the Guidi.

The plan was that Sheila would spend her days painting, while I would sit and reflect on the fact that I'd not worked for years, had an infant daughter, and was unable to produce or even reflect on anything that I or anyone else would consider useful.

Sitting in the quiet of the piazza that first day, half an hour into my coffee, I felt the plan working. My thoughts, quite on their own, had ventured into matters of my life that I'd long ignored.

There is no telling how far this would have taken me had I not noticed that the old men, who had been lined up opposite me against the wall on the south side of the piazza, were now standing, in exactly the same order, against the west wall. As the sun moved across the sky, the men followed the shade.

Waiting for the men to reach my table—the break I needed from my self-reflection—I realized that we would have no way of communicating. According to Sheila, no one in the town spoke English, and I spoke no Italian.

Two hours later, I was surrounded. The men and I stared at each other for several minutes; then one of them asked—in lightly scrambled English—if I was interested in an *Etrusco*. I accepted.

The man entered the café and quickly reappeared with two glasses of a luminous orange fluid. As we drank, I mentioned my surprise at his ability to speak English.

The old man explained that while others in the town spoke no English, those over eighty could carry on a conversation. As soldiers in World War II, they had been captured by the Allies and shipped to prisons in England or South Africa. During the day, the men were released into nearby villages, where they worked on farms or in factories, replacing the men who were at war. The Italians fell in love with the local women and learned to speak English.

These men told me their stories and became my friends.

I was an oddity in Sutri—an American and a man of working age who also followed the shade around the square. The absence of tourists, American or otherwise, is endemic to the area.

The area, known popularly as "Tuscia" (the Romans referred to the Etruscans as Etrusci or Tusci), extends from Rome in the south to Tuscany in the north, the Tyrrhenian Sea in the west to Umbria in the east. The largest city in the region is Viterbo, with a population of approximately 60,000. Sutri is an equal distance between Viterbo and Rome.

The people of Tuscia—quiet, unassuming, and suspicious of foreigners—are not suited to the kind of self-promotion that is necessary to attract foreign tourists and that comes so easily to other regions in Italy. There is also the problem that the important antiquities in the region are Etruscan, a culture that remains largely impenetrable to scholars (the Etruscan language has yet to be translated), let alone the weekend tourist.

As a result, Tuscia is one of the great, yet neglected,

areas in Italy. This despite the fact its beauty is equal to that of any region in Italy—medieval towns perched on hilltops, volcanic lakes, abandoned beaches, and mountains forested with chestnut and oak trees.

It took me a month or two before I realized that the waiter and waitress at the Guidi Caffè, a clean and welcoming pair, were Gino and Dina Guidi and that they owned not only the café but also a good part of the rest of Sutri.

Despite their status, the Guidis spend their days serving coffee and pastries in the square. Dina, who is in her fifties, is one of the most refined women in the town. Elegantly dressed, she is in the café at seven in the morning with her husband, her apron on, handing the people of the town, her friends, their first espresso. Every other day, she and Gino are replaced by Gino's brother, Enzo, and his wife, Nilla.

In the evenings, Dina, Gino, and the extended family, all handsome and entertaining, sit outside, having a drink, offering a chair to anyone who wants to have a coffee or simply needs to sit. The Guidis are the grand family of Sutri.

The Guidis' home is a Renaissance palazzo that rises directly across the piazza from their café. It is, by any standard, magnificent—four stories tall, with a massive neoclassical façade, and views of the hills, pastures, and ruins that surround the town.

Not long after our arrival, Sheila and I were invited by Dina to have dinner at her home. The dinner, Dina insisted, would be informal.

The dinner—prepared and served by Dina—was a seven-course affair, which included arugula layered with sliced Parmesan; bresaola; stuffed tomatoes; baked zucchini; fettuccine with wild boar sauce; pork roast wrapped in pastry; and for dessert, chilled grapes and watermelon slathered with fresh whipped cream and liqueur. Pastries from the Guidis' pastry shop (located on the first floor of their palazzo) were offered with the coffee.

The most unusual dish was a traditional Sutrian recipe of beans in a sauce of tomatoes and boiled pigskins. The beans were the local "fagioli regina." The fagioli regina are dense and bulbous and taste of chestnuts. They are considered to be the finest bean in Italy. Every year Sutri hosts a bean festival in honor of the fagioli regina. The Blessing of the Bean, as performed by the local clergy, begins the festival.

The dining room at the Guidi palazzo overlooks the Piazza del Comune. During dinner, Dina described how Gino, the son of a poor family, had grown up in a small apartment on the piazza. Owing to his affection for the square, Gino acquired property in and around the square at a time when few were interested in the central piazzas of old Italian towns. As the value of real estate in the old towns increased, Gino and his family grew wealthy.

As I listened to this, it struck me that the Guidi Caffè was located in one of the few buildings in the square that was not owned by the Guidi family. Gino explained why this was so.

The site where the café is now located was originally occupied by a collection of small, undistinguished buildings. In the 1920s, a fellow known as Old Man Mezzadonna bought up all the buildings, razed them all, and began construction on a palazzo that he intended to be the finest in Sutri. After three months, and with the palazzo half built, all construction halted. When days passed and there was still no sign that work would resume, the people in the town began to gossip. They agreed that Old Man Mezzadonna had run out of money.

Word got back to Mezzadonna, who ordered that the workers return to the square. He would not have people believe that he had run out of money.

As work resumed the townspeople realized that the workers were not finishing the palazzo but tearing it down. After a week and a day, the entire building was gone; and a pyramid of rubble sat where there was once a beautiful, albeit half-finished, palazzo.

Time passed and no effort was made to remove the debris. Then one morning, the people of the town woke to an amazing sight: the entire square was filled with bottles of wine. Not dozens of bottles, not hundreds of bottles, but thousands of bottles, and not local wine, but rare, expensive wine with exotic labels.

As everyone gathered to see the square, the workers returned. It was at this point that Old Man Mezzadonna climbed to the top of the rubble.

"Rebuild the palazzo," he commanded the workers in a voice that could be heard throughout the square. "And build it," he continued, "according to the same plan that you used before. Not a single detail is to be changed, except one: this time, you will use wine, not water, in the concrete."

When the young Gino Guidi was told this story by his father, he vowed that if he was ever wealthy enough to open a bar in Sutri, he would do so in the palazzo made of wine.

The Blessing of the Bean

THE morning after my meal at the Guidis', I was not well and stayed in bed.

When my condition improved slightly, I attempted a stroll outside my house. Passing down via Eugenio Agneni, crossing in front of the bakery, and heading south toward the Porta Vecchia, I was just outside the front door of the city archive when I was jolted by an intestinal phenomenon that compelled me to brace myself against a wall so as not to fall. Whatever there was of my will (or of those involuntary reflexes that in a time of crisis allow a child to pick up a car) had given way to the force that had seized my interior.

Not knowing a doctor but remembering that there was

a pharmacy next to the Guidi Caffè, I began a slow and contorted walk toward the square. With each step my pain grew.

As I entered the square, a young woman, possibly from the pharmacy, intercepted me. When I muttered that at least one relative had died of stomach cancer and that my father was afflicted with ulcers throughout his life, she took me to the Guidi and sat me upright under an umbrella. In the meantime, she phoned a cab to take me to the nearest hospital.

That hospital was in Ronciglione, which meant that it would take the cab at least thirty minutes to get to Sutri and then another twenty to the hospital. As I waited, a short elderly man with a full head of black hair appeared before me.

There was no need and perhaps no time to wait for a taxi, the old man explained. Holding me with one of his arms, he led me out of the square and down an alley toward a small parking lot in front of the Cathedral of S. Maria Assunta. Stopping to prop me up against the side of his car, a Fiat 500, he began searching for his keys.

But he was not searching for his keys and it was not his car.

Before I knew it, his arms were wrapped around my

legs. Grabbing my knees from behind, he pushed me face first up onto the hood of the car. The weight of my body, propelled against the rounded hood of the car, forced my abdomen into my spinal column and rib cage. What issued forth was a vaporous cataclysm, a gaseous exorcism, of such enormity that it echoed throughout the square.

Still on top of the hood, my head and body nearly cleared of pain, I caught sight of the old man scaling the side of the car. Intending to finish what he had started, he was within seconds of hurling his muscular rump down on my back. I rolled off the hood and onto the pavement.

Ladies from the church—having left their afternoon prayers to locate the source of the noise—gathered over my body; just above their heads hovered the old man. Attempting to clear the way for his final leap, he assured the ladies that the cause of my difficulties was nothing but the inadvertent consumption of more fagioli regina than a newcomer to Sutri could be expected to handle, possibly even survive. The women nodded; they understood.

My crisis had passed. Over the next months, my body would adapt to my surroundings and gradually I was able to consume more than a couple of the fagioli regina at a time. With instruction from the local citizens, I developed a sense of the relative strengths of different varieties of

beans and the degree to which various methods of prepa-
ration increased or diminished their effect. That said, I
will not go to a meal in Sutri without taking note of the
nearest Fiat 500.

The old man who had rescued me from my discomfort
was a farmer, and through him I met other farmers. One
of them, a man named Vittore, was retired and consequently, with his days free, a regular at the Guidi.

Vittore grew up outside of Sutri, on land his family has
been farming for as long as anyone could remember.
Because Vittore's father needed him to work the fields, he
pulled the boy out of school when he was thirteen.

When Vittore's friends grew up and left their farms, he
stayed home with his father and mother. When others in
the town encouraged him to join the Fascists, he couldn't
be troubled. And when men from the village volunteered
to fight, he told them he didn't like to fight. His body was
short, his arms long, and his hands wide—wrong for a sol-
dier but perfect for a farmer.

War became inescapable. Drafted and sent to northern
Africa, he was captured in Libya. The English forced
Vittore and other Italian soldiers to march from Libya to

Egypt. Two weeks of continuous walking caused the prisoners to wear through their socks. When the English refused to provide new socks and the temperatures reached 100 degrees, Vittore's feet began to bleed and the skin drop off. The bleeding stopped when the leather of his shoes replaced the skin of his feet. In Egypt, as the shoes were stripped off, his feet were exposed to the bone.

After spending time in a prison camp in Cairo, Vittore was transferred to South Africa. From there, he was shipped to Liverpool. The guards on the boat were sailors whose ships or submarines had been sunk by the Germans. The guards used any excuse to take their revenge on the prisoners.

A cousin was on the boat with Vittore. One day they were playing with a ball that they had found on the boat. When the ball rolled into a restricted area, Vittore's cousin caught the attention of a guard. The guard waved him into the restricted zone. As Vittore's cousin went after the ball, the guard shot him.

Over the course of the journey, food and water began to run out. The prisoners began to die. Vittore decided that he "wasn't going to let the English kill him," and when the boat landed in southern England, with dozens dead and the rest crippled by disease or exhaustion, Vittore alone walked off the boat unassisted. Once in England, he was assigned to a farm. It was there that he learned to speak English.

In 1946, Vittore was allowed to return to Italy. Not long thereafter, he met a woman from Sutri whom he immediately knew he would wed—her name was Rosa. Vittore and Rosa were married in the church of S. Silvestro, and Rosa moved onto Vittore's farm.

At around this time, Vittore decided to plant a crop of beans.

Every day Vittore rose at three in the morning to water the beans. When the watering was completed, he would spend the rest of the day planting or harvesting, depending on the season. Because fagioli regina do not mature at the same time, those who are serious about them, such as Vittore, subject themselves to the backbreaking process of walking the fields, finding the beans that are ready to be consumed, and plucking them from the plant by hand.

Vittore and Rosa raised the best crop of fagioli regina in Sutri. But what Vittore liked most about them were their colors: pearls encased in a bright pink, marbleized shell.

But as the years passed, Vittore found that his beans were of interest to fewer and fewer people. People didn't appreciate the distinctions between varieties of beans, didn't know when a bean was too ripe to be eaten, didn't care about their color. Moreover, few people, other than Rosa, were willing to get up with Vittore to do the watering at three in the morning or walk the fields or pick and shuck the beans by hand.

When Rosa died, Vittore was left alone on the farm.

When even the shops in Sutri stopped selling his beans, he left his land.

Today Vittore sits in the square. He never remarried. When I asked about his life, he spoke at length about the beans he once raised and the town that failed to appreciate them. He points out, with some resentment, that his beans have never been included in the bean festival.

Nearly eight months after my first conversation with Vittore and shortly before the bean festival, I asked one of the organizers about Vittore's beans. The man insisted that Vittore's beans had been excluded from the festival for reasons other than their quality. The real problem, he claimed, was something that he was not prepared to discuss.

Both Vittore and the organizer of the annual bean festival were telling the truth. Vittore was right to say that people in Sutri were less concerned about the quality and variety of beans than they used to be; he was also right to say that few people in the town were willing to put in the effort necessary to plant and harvest the beans.

But the fellow from the bean festival also had a point, though one that politeness prevented him from saying: Vittore's beans were just too potent. When I asked Vittore about the power of his beans over those that are currently grown in the town, Vittore stood up and pointed to the other bean farmers in the square: "They can't handle my beans. When you eat their beans, you 'talk' in your sleep; when you eat my beans, you have to sleep with your ass out the window."

The Hand

THE palazzo made of wine is now occupied by two men: Aurellio and Alberto Mezzadonna, descendants of Old Man Mezzadonna.

Aurellio Mezzadonna rarely leaves his palazzo, and when he does it is to step just a few feet beyond the front door and then retreat.

Every day he wears the same outfit: a floor-length, blue silk dressing gown, no shirt, and a detachable wing collar. The collar is fastened to the dressing gown by a large, silver pin. Because the gown is never removed, its backside contains a precise and soiled record of the deterioration of Aurellio's skeleton over the last decades.

He wears knee-high red rubber boots and a soft black

fisherman's hat pulled over his eyes. His left arm, wrist to elbow, is heavy with filigreed gold and silver bracelets. In his left hand he holds a riding crop. His right hand is covered by a stiff black glove.

I first saw him one day as I was sitting at the Guidi. He was walking in front of his palazzo, and after every couple of steps he would stop and look up into the sun. Unhappy with what he saw, he would move on. He repeated this several times before coming to a full stop. Reaching into his pocket, the riding crop dangling from his wrist, he pulled out a cigarette and wedged it in between two fingers of the glove. Returning to his pocket, he removed a second object, which flashed in the sunlight. Checking the sun again, he held the object above his glove. Seconds later, a flame burst from the glove.

He had lit his cigarette with a magnifying glass.

While I was staring at this, the man at the table next to me leaned over and asked if I'd noticed anything "odd about Mezzadonna."

Odd about Mezzadonna? What was not odd about Mezzadonna?

Deciding from the look on my face that I was not going to give him the right answer, the man whispered, "The hand . . . the hand."

The hand with the riding crop?

"Of course not. The other hand." It was clear that he thought I was an imbecile.

That hand, I felt obligated to point out, was impossible to see since it was covered by a black glove.

"That's the point," the man retorted. "Mezzadonna doesn't take off the glove, because everyone would see that he doesn't have a hand."

If he doesn't have a hand, what was under the glove?

"A cat's paw."

What did he mean by a "cat's paw"?

"A cat's paw," he explained slowly, "is the foot of a cat, covered on one side with fur and on the other with a thick padding and short, sharp claws." Mezzadonna—and the man had no doubt about this—was possessed of a cat's paw, complete with the claws.

As to the red rubber boots, a woman at the Guidi provided the explanation: "Each night Aurellio goes to the basement of his palazzo and rows on the High Seas," which also, I imagined, explained the fisherman's cap. The Guidis hear the rowing noises in their café.

Aurellio is old and his shoulders are stooped. Because he has rarely been in the sun, his skin is perfectly white and unwrinkled; his features are delicate. The fisherman's cap covers what little hair he has. At first glance his gender is unclear. With the robe, the bracelets, and the delicacy of his features, he could quite easily be mistaken for an old woman.

When I commented to one of the regulars at the Guidi on such a man having the name Mezzadonna, I was told that Mezzadonna was not an uncommon name around Sutri and that there were not only Mezzadonnas but also Mezzauomos and even Mezzauovos. The last of the Half-Eggs, the man regretted to report, had passed away just a month before.

The other inhabitant of the Mezzadonna palazzo is Aurellio's brother, Alberto. He is as sociable as Aurellio is reclusive. I've yet to pass Alberto that he's not invited me for a smoke and an espresso. At almost any time of day, Alberto can be found at the tobacco shop or in one of the cafés in the square talking to a crowd of his friends. One of the reasons for Alberto's popularity is that he is known to have supernatural powers—powers that he harnesses solely for the good of the town.

While Alberto is willing to deploy his power to assist the residents of Sutri with nearly all requests, he specializes in the laying of hands on tractor engines. There is a mechanic on the road leading into Rome who frequently makes use of Alberto's gifts. Driving in and out of Sutri, I often catch Alberto standing over a tractor, his hands moving gently across the hood while the mechanic, wrench at his side, looks on in wonder.

I have heard the opinion, widely held in town, that the behavior of the Mezzadonnas may be explained by generations of inbreeding—a practice that the Mezzadonnas hit upon as a means of keeping their assets within the family. Even now it is reported that the family is attempting to convince one of the remaining Mezzadonnas to marry his first cousin. The young man has balked at the idea, but the family has continued to insist. It is said that the family is having trouble understanding his objection.

The Postman

THE first time I saw him—a rotund, middle-aged man with a slack face, glistening red eyes, and a lively black mole—he was riding his motor scooter sidesaddle through the Piazza del Comune. Following just behind him, attempting to avoid detection, was a crowd of people on foot.

Most arresting to me was neither the man nor those following him, but the scooter. Ten years ago, someone—no one remembers who—made a decision that would forever change the town: the Piazza del Comune would be closed to traffic—a decision that would distinguish the central square in Sutri from all others in the region.

The owner of the local bookstore explained that the

man was allowed to ride his scooter in the square because he was the village postman. When I commented that I needed to speak with him about my mail, the owner of the bookstore replied that I might well be wasting my time since the postman was illiterate.

While I had no idea whether the postman was illiterate, in Sutri it was not a burden: with everyone passing each other in the piazza three or four times a day, misdelivered letters are easily redistributed. If a letter is important, those waiting for the letter will follow the postman around until he takes his morning coffee and then, while he is inside the café, rifle through his bag.

The next time I saw the postman, it was at a restaurant on the shores of Lake Vico, just outside Ronciglione. Lake Vico sits in the crater of what was once a volcano. The restaurant has outdoor tables facing the lake, and it was at one of these tables that I spotted the postman. In front of him on the table were pieces of bread pinned under a sauce of a dark green color.

I asked the waiter about the dish. He responded proudly, "The Bruschetta of Herod—the speciality of the house—made from the algae of Lake Vico."

When I later discussed the bruschetta with the owner of the restaurant, a handsome man with a grave manner, he conceded that despite the reputation enjoyed by the Bruschetta of Herod, there was not a drop of algae in it. The dish came about when, just before the restaurant opened, he was approached by his brother, who at the time was referring to himself as Herod and whom the owner believed to be mad. Herod insisted that if the restaurant offered a bruschetta made of algae from Lake Vico, the restaurant would be an immediate success.

The owner dismissed the idea as repulsive and preposterous, sending Herod off with a warning not to return.

A week later, Herod was back. This time he brought with him the "algae" sauce, a viscous concoction of green olives, artichokes, and capers. When his brother sampled it and declared that it was not what he imagined algae to taste like, Herod scoffed: the restaurant's proximity to the lake and people's fantasies would convince them that they were eating algae. To pacify his sibling (and keep him away from the restaurant), the owner agreed to serve a bruschetta covered, or so the menu would claim, in the algae of Lake Vico. Hence, the "Bruschetta of Herod."

The dish caused a great deal of talk, and people came from all over to eat at the restaurant. Today the restaurant supports not only Herod's brother, but Herod's mother, sister-in-law, and various other members of the family.

On my way out of the restaurant, I was stopped by the owner. He held out a photograph. The photograph, he told me, was taken at the carnival sponsored each year by the town of Ronciglione. As part of the carnival, there is a parade featuring floats constructed by local civic and religious groups.

But neither the carnival nor the parade explains the thousands who come to the celebration. They come in the hope of seeing one person—Herod.

A few years ago, when towns in the area decided to crack down on bordellos, he arrived in a contraption entitled "Float in Honor of the Assumption of the Madams," with the corpulent Herod lying on a chaise longue and wearing a gown, makeup, and a wig.

The photograph which I was shown by the owner of the restaurant was taken years later, at a different parade. Herod had come as an enormous black butterfly. The photograph was of Herod draped in black cloth, his face covered by a black mask, and his wings a glowing expanse of orange and yellow.

Instead of being driven down the parade route, Herod walked it very slowly and very carefully—and as the people of the town watched him they knew that were Herod to take the slightest wrong step, Death would come to the town—not in the future but right then, as they watched the parade, as they held the hands of their children. And they and the entire parade stopped, for no one dared to disturb Herod.

As I left the restaurant, the postman was still sitting at his table. Turning to the owner of the restaurant I inquired whether locals, such as the postman, were aware that there was no algae in the bruschetta.

"No need to tell him," the owner responded. "He's the one who created it."

The Piazza

THE Piazza del Comune—the square that is the center of Sutri—is not a square but a rectangle. The entrance to the piazza is a Roman arch built of blocks of peperino, a light volcanic stone formed of sand. The blocks were carved by the Romans in the second century A.D.

The age of the blocks causes little comment from the locals since the town dates back to the late Bronze Age— approximately 1000 B.C. The official stamps of the town refer to it as the "Very Ancient City of Sutri," and the town claims to be one of the oldest Italian towns in continuous existence.

The buildings on the square, with the exception of

the Mezzadonna palazzo, were constructed between the sixteenth and eighteenth centuries. The oldest of these structures are the private homes, which flank the arch. Since the Mezzadonna palazzo is built in the style of the other buildings on the square, the square is a perfect Renaissance piazza.

Directly opposite the Mezzadonna palazzo is the Palazzo Comunale, once the residence of Principe Urbano del Drago and now the seat of the municipal government. Del Drago kept his horses stabled behind the palazzo, with an alley leading from the square to the stables.

In the middle of the Piazza del Comune sits a fountain. The square's original fountain was sold and is now rumored to be in Florida. The water in the new fountain tastes quite good—as does the water throughout the region—and families come with buckets. Many say that it is the water in Sutri that accounts for the unusual longevity of its people.

The shops in the square include one trattoria, one bread shop, a bank, hair parlor, tobacco store, jewelry shop, cheese and sausage shop, laundry, general store, the "Pro Loco," the "Emporio," and three cafés.

The trattoria—Sfera d'Oro—is located on the ground floor of the Guidi palazzo. The trattoria features tables outside, and each morning a newspaper is spread out on one of them. The old men of the square stand over that paper one after another to have their turn with it, and then, when each is done, they back off to allow others their time. When they have all finished, they stand in a circle and argue over what they have read.

Sfera d'Oro serves a bird known as *gallina faraona*. Native to Africa, the bird was introduced to Europe in the sixteenth century by way of Egypt, which explains why it is referred to as "the hen of the pharaohs" or "African pheasant." With an unusually strong flavor, the bird is popular throughout Sutri, but it is Sfera d'Oro that does the best job with it.

The sauce served with the *faraona* is a combination of olive oil, garlic, pepper, anchovies, capers, and chicken livers. The cooks at the Sfera d'Oro are two large, joyous women, who can be seen sitting outside the trattoria at the end of the day. In addition to *faraona*, they make an unequaled *pappardelle alla lepre* (a wide pasta with a sauce of wild hare), a dish served throughout the region.

The bread shop shares the ground floor of the Guidi palazzo with Sfera d'Oro. The Guidi palazzo was originally a seminary, and the bread shop served as the chapel for the seminarians. It was Gino Guidi's idea to convert the chapel into a bread shop. At the time he bought the palazzo, Gino was convinced that the one thing missing from the square was a place to buy bread. The piazza had cafés and restaurants (businesses that depend on bread) and people living in and around the square who bought fresh bread once or twice a day, but no shop on the square that sold bread.

Gino's instincts were right; from its first day the bread shop was popular.

When I remarked on his talent for starting businesses, Gino told me this story:

Having decided upon a bread shop, Gino was faced with the considerable task of stripping and removing from the chapel its pews, lamps, lectern, and other fixtures. As luck would have it, Gino met a man in the square who was prepared to do this for a fee.

With the chapel emptied, the walls repainted, the equipment installed, and a baker on premises, the bread shop was ready for business. When the bread shop opened, there was a story in the local paper reporting the event. Gino Guidi, proud of his accomplishment, pointed out the article to Dina.

But it was not the article about the bread shop that

caught Dina's eye. What Dina saw was a much smaller item on the same page: the announcement of an auction at which the public would be allowed the opportunity to purchase rare artifacts from a Renaissance chapel—a chapel that had been located in the central piazza of Sutri. When Gino confessed that he had given the contents of the chapel away for nothing (omitting the detail that he had actually paid the man to take it away), Dina was furious, insisting that Gino go to the auction and buy something as a reminder of the important chapel that was once on their property.

At the auction, the items from the chapel went for much more than anyone expected, and Gino, desperate to find something to bring back to his wife, decided on a small section of the pews. Even this, however, was of interest to those at the auction, and by the time the bidding was over, Gino had spent a good deal of money on the pew.

Once home, Gino presented the pew to his wife and children. After carefully examining it, Dina inquired how much her husband had spent on it. When he told her, she looked again at the pew and then quietly addressed him. "Well, Gino, at least one thing is clear from all of this." "Yes?" Gino Guidi replied, pleased to know that something positive resulted from his efforts. "You are," she confided, "an even bigger fool than I thought you were."

The shop in the square that is the most difficult to define is the "Emporio." The ever-present figure behind the counter, Lello, is the proprietor. In addition to pens, scissors, rosaries, and pads of paper, Lello sells buttons, hats, socks, and shirts, not to mention an extensive inventory of hair products. Lello also offers a first-class collection of brassieres, garter belts, and other undergarments from the 1930s and '40s. Of these, his pride and joy are the silk stockings that dangle directly above the counter, giving the impression that antennae are sprouting from Lello's bald head.

On the counter at the Emporio—just next to the cash register—are bags filled with pasta in the shape of male genitalia, complete with scrota.

Hanging outside the shop, next to the entrance, is a pair of lady's panties that are three feet across and two feet high. So gigantic are these panties that people entering the store appear to be crawling through the crotch of the panties—a through-the-looking-glass experience enhanced by the sight of Lello, his antennae, and the thousand scrota.

The piazza's barbershop is located between the Pro Loco and Sfera d'Oro. There is another barbershop down the street. There are two barbers in Sutri: Marco and Paolo. While Marco is an expert hair cutter and there is no doubt that he cares about each of his customers, there is one aspect of Marco's artistry that might be considered a limitation: he knows only one haircut. It is the style that female cabaret singers wear in their later years—the intelligent, stylish, just-released-from-rehab look—the prison cut with a little extra on the top.

Marco has mastered this hairdo and it is this style that he gives to anyone who comes in the door, regardless of age or sex. This hairstyle is the identifying characteristic of everyone, including myself, who lives in Sutri. I call it the "Marco."

Next to to the barbershop is the Pro Loco, a government tourist office that occupies the ground floor of the offices of the municipal government. Since the number of tourists who visit Sutri is minuscule, the Pro Loco is rarely busy.

The few foreign tourists who visit Sutri run into the problem that no one in the Pro Loco speaks a language other than Italian. If a tourist doesn't happen to speak Italian, the man behind the desk at the Pro Loco yells something to the effect of "What the hell are you doing here if you don't speak Italian and how do you expect to find your way around this city?" If this doesn't succeed in getting the tourist to speak Italian or at least scare the tourist out of the office, the man throws up his hands, storms out the door, and takes a seat at the Tonetti Caffè, located next door to the Pro Loco. To calm his nerves, he orders a drink.

During the day, drinks at the Tonetti are served by Maria and Lucia, the owners of the café. In the evenings the women are assisted by a man known as The Sixth.

Maria and Lucia are said to have a profound interest in other people's business. Bruce Johnston, a journalist for the *Daily Telegraph*, tells the story of how, shortly after his divorce, he was sitting at the Tonetti when Maria approached his table. After setting down his coffee, she announced that the problem with Bruce's marriage was his mother-in-law. "The outrageous thing about this," Bruce told me, "is that other than ordering coffee, I had never spoken to Maria.

"Worse," he added, "she was right."

The social structure of the piazza is as fixed as its architecture.

On the outside of the square, sitting on the stone

benches just in front of the buildings, are the old men, the guardians of the square. Though not one of them is well-off, they make a point of wearing sports jackets and pressed shirts when they visit the square. They speak quietly to each other but most of their days are spent in silence, watching others. Occasionally one of the men will sing or whistle and the others will join him. When they leave the square for meals, they lock arms. Though many need wheelchairs, none uses one.

Funerals, regardless of the social standing of the deceased, pass through the square. As soon as the chanting of the mourners is heard, the owners of the stores in the square pull their gates shut, and as the procession enters the square (always on foot), everyone in the square rises. All remain standing until the last member of the cortege has passed.

The center of the square is the province of the children. They play in the fountain, sit on the edge of it, ride their bicycles around it.

In the space between the children and the old men, in between the walls and fountain, are the sons and daughters of the old men, the parents of the children. They sit at the café tables, taking in the sun, enjoying the company of their friends.

I encountered three people for whom the structure of

the square has no meaning. One is a woman no more than thirty-five years old. Attractive and extremely well turned out, she stands in the center of the square, removes a pack of cigarettes from her handbag, and then, with the first draw, begins slowly goose-stepping to the outside edge of the square. She checks each step to make certain that it lands precisely in front of the last. She is tightrope-walking across the square, each foot set carefully in front of the other so as not to fall off the edge of her walk.

I watched her for months before I was told her story.

The rumor is that she came from elsewhere and was involved with someone who beat her. One beating so damaged her brain that she never recovered. Run out of other towns, she found her way to Sutri. She lived alone, never marrying.

People in Sutri treat her respectfully, and no one suggests that she be removed—on the contrary, everyone makes certain that her path is clear and that her story is told.

Another woman walks the square but she avoids the center. She moves between the shops on the perimeter, but never stops to enter. Her daughter drowned in a river not far from Sutri, I learned. Her husband, unable to contain his grief, threw himself into the same river.

The other person in the town for whom the social structure of the square is irrelevant is Don Erri. Dressed in black, his posture rigid, standing taller than any other man in town, and with a massive girth, he is by far the most intimidating figure in Sutri.

Don Erri is rarely seen sitting in the square. If he passes through, he will speak to any person who stops him, but he does not linger; he is never seen in the cafés or the trattoria. His domain is the Piazza Duomo (just east of the Piazza del Comune), so named because it is the site of the Cathedral of S. Maria Assunta. He is the priest of S. Maria Assunta. For Don Erri, the Piazza del Comune represents a civic order that is separate from and not wholly in harmony with the order to which Don Erri is committed.

The Piazza Duomo, though the quietest of the three main squares in Sutri, is the richest historically. Because of Sutri's proximity to Rome and because it was the first town to come under the possession of the pope (the town was gifted to Pope Gregory III by the Longobard king Liutprando in A.D. 725), Sutri became a place of retreat for the popes, particularly when they were under attack elsewhere (as was Pope Eugenius III when, in 1146, he fled to Sutri to escape a popular revolt in Rome).

Located to the west of the Piazza del Comune (almost the same distance as the Piazza Duomo to the east), the Piazza Cavour contains an empty fountain and just a few tables. The people who occupy those tables appear to be in a constant state of brooding.

The spirit of the Piazza Cavour permeates the via Roma, the street which begins at the main gate of the old city (the Porta Maroni), passes through the Piazza Cavour, and ends at the central square. On the via Roma are a collection of merchants, including butchers, fabric makers, vegetable sellers, a bridal shop, cheese venders, and a shoe salesman. The via Roma is narrow, and the shops draw quite a few people. Moreover, there is no sidewalk on the via Roma, so with the traffic and the people, the road is treacherous. No one lingers on the via Roma.

No one, that is, except the woman who owns the shoe store. The woman with the sparkling red hair. She does not hesitate to pull her stool out in front of her shop and sit there, in the middle of traffic, visiting with whoever passes by. If she is not on her stool in front of her shop, she is across the street on the same stool, also in the traffic.

Over lunch with Vittore one afternoon, I noticed his shoes and I asked him whether he had bought them from the woman down the street.

"What woman?"

Vittore was genuinely puzzled.

"The one who owns the shoe store."

"Frank owns the shoe store," Vittore corrected me.

Now I was confused.

"If Frank owns the shoe store," I asked, "who is the woman?"

"Frank."

Vittore was not the only one. It was soon clear to me that everyone in town was under the impression that the owner of the shoe store was a man. Or was it something else: Were the people of this town so malleable that they could accept, even come to believe, that a woman had changed her sex by doing nothing more than referring to herself as Frank?

My interest in this did not last long and I would have forgotten it had I not, one Thursday morning on my way to the open market, crossed in front of the woman at the shoe store. As I passed her, I caught myself thinking that she was a little taller than most of the women in Sutri, had a shade more hair on her face, and exhibited a beauty that was more hale than delicate. It also occurred to me that I'd never seen her in a dress. And at this point she ceased being a woman in my mind and became a man. She had jumped categories.

I was content with this and even decided that at the first opportunity I would refer to her as a man.

That opportunity presented itself the next week, when a friend came to visit. He had lived in Sutri, and over dinner with Sheila and me, he discussed some of the people in town whom he had known. When I mentioned Frank, my friend rolled his eyes.

"You are not going to tell me that Frank is a woman," I begged.

"No."

"What, then?"

"A half-and-half."

My mind returned to an evening many years before. I was in New York and having drinks with Herbert Huncke, who lived upstairs from me in the Chelsea Hotel. Huncke, a Beat writer, then in his eighties, took the opportunity of our conversation to tell me that his most thrilling companion had been a hermaphrodite from Chicago by the name of Elsie-John. True hermaphrodites, Huncke educated me, are extremely rare ("having the outer *and* *inner* organs of the male and female").

But it was not the sexual bounty that drew Herbert to Elsie-John; it was her beauty—a beauty that was "neither male nor female," he told me.

With this conversation in mind, I asked my friend

whether anyone in Sutri actually knew that Frank was a hermaphrodite. My friend replied that though no one knew Frank in a sexual way ("The tragedy of Frank is that he is blessed with two sexes but is a virgin in both"), people in Sutri had more reliable sources of information. I left it at that.

There is a girl in Sutri by the name of Angela. I met her through her older sister, Carolina, who looked after our daughter.

For her whole life, Angela was every bit her name, a cherub with a plump, innocent face framed by long spirals of light hair. If there is a name that everyone in Sutri knows, it's Angela's.

Angela's mother and father are Guatemalan, and they brought Angela and Carolina to Sutri when Angela was just a child. Because the girls spoke no Italian, Angela's mother, Mina, accompanied the girls when they walked through the town or played in the square.

Frank would go out of his way to greet Mina and her daughters. The odd thing was that Frank would refer to Angela as "Maria." Frank had no trouble with "Mina" or "Carolina," but Angela was always "Maria."

Each time that Frank called Angela by the wrong name—which was every time he saw her—Mina made a point of correcting him. "My daughter's name is Angela, not Maria," she declared. But it would make no difference. Frank continued to call her Maria.

One afternoon, when Mina, Carolina, and Angela were shopping on the via Roma, Frank called out to them, referring again to Angela as "Maria." Stopping in the middle of the street, the four-year-old Angela shouted back, "So, if I'm Maria, you tell me what you are: man or woman."

Throwing up his arms, Frank shouted, "I don't know!"

Carolina, who recounted the story of her sister's confrontation with Frank, concluded by remarking that despite having been raised in Guatemala—with its shamans, animal sacrifices, spirits, and black magic— nothing had prepared her for Sutri.

If I had a place in the square, it was with the old men. We met every day and I was the recipient of their kindness. They would read to me from Ariosto. They would take care of my daughter. Men who had little means would prepare lavish dinners for my family—toasted bread with boar pâté, pasta blanketed in sliced truffles, fresh fish from Lake Bracciano. They taught Sheila Italian. And when she exhibited her paintings, they all turned out.

As I watched the old men from across the square or the dinner table, something happened: they were joined by other old men—dressed differently but the same sort of men. But when I asked about them, no one knew these men. They seemed to belong to the square but had never before been there.

These were the old men from my childhood; they were my grandparents and great-uncles and their friends. They had exotic names—Milo, Maynard, Doc, Harlan, J. J.— and they would come from all parts of the Midwest to sit in our home in Nebraska and drink and gamble and tell stories of their lives in the small towns from which they came. As a child, I was engrossed by them.

As I grew older, however, I came to view them differently: these men were the eccentrics of their towns— adorned in silk suits and dressing gowns, carrying walking sticks, and having no families or apparent means of support—they were the debauched oddities about whom others in the town whispered. But my great-uncles and -aunts always returned to their hometowns, and I came to wonder why; and as well, how it was that those towns endured them.

When the last of my great-uncles died, I went back for the funeral. Days later my mother and I were at a restaurant when I overheard a conversation at the next table. A woman was telling the story of a family in which one of four brothers announced over an otherwise uneventful dinner that he was moving to the basement and would not be seen again. Accommodating his son's desire, the father constructed a room and a system of electronic signals so that the son could be notified when his food was being brought down.

The son kept to his pledge and was not seen again.

The story was a good one and I started to jot it down. It was then that I realized that my mother had stopped eating. And I stopped writing. The story was being told about my parents and one of my brothers, the one who disappeared when I was eight. Despite my belief that we were utterly conventional (unlike my older relatives), the people at the next table were talking about us in the way that I was just talking about the Mezzadonnas. We were, it seems, the Mezzadonnas of Nebraska.

The Philosopher

ARRIVING in Sutri, we moved into a house, a former granary that sits at the edge of a cliff on the northern end of the town. Erosion has left part of the house suspended without support over the cliff.

Beneath the house, at the bottom of the cliff, is a hazelnut grove. The orchard is owned by a young woman, Fiorina. When her father died, she took over the orchard. To the delight of everyone in the town, who thought the job of raising and processing hazelnuts was too much for such a young woman, she took up exactly where her father had left off.

When I first met Fiorina, it was autumn and she was in the process of collecting and preparing the hazelnuts for market. During the day she would drive her tractor through the fields loading hazelnuts, and at the end of the day, haul them to a shed at the edge of the orchard. Inside the shed is a giant roaster. Fiorina would devote her evenings to feeding it hazelnuts. The heat from the roaster separates the hazelnuts from their shells.

Fiorina's hazelnuts make their way into various local products, including candies and *tozzetti*, a hard cookie that is sold throughout Sutri. In other places, *tozzetti* are dipped into coffee, but in Sutri, this is not done. Espressos in Sutri contain such a small amount of liquid that the coffee would be completely absorbed into the *tozzetti;* but the other reason is that dipping the *tozzetti* in coffee would be an insult to the appearance of the hazelnut, so perfectly revealed in its toasted bread.

Never did I sense that Fiorina was overwhelmed by her efforts. She seemed pleased with herself. What's more, she found inspiration. The shells of the hazelnuts, Fiorina believed, could be used in a fireplace as an alternative to wood. This would cut the cost of energy to people in the town.

As I stared from the house over the tops of the hazelnut trees, something astonishing occurred to me. Never before conscious of Nature, I grew preoccupied by it. Trees surrounded the house, vines scaled its walls, pink roses embroidered its paths. In the late afternoons, birds glided in and out of the windows. I spent days writing in my journals about this small corner of Nature that I was so fortunate to encounter. Since it was the end of summer, I became aware of the exquisite decay that begins at that time. When I was through describing the area around the house, I would move on to contiguous area, and when that was done, on to another, moving farther out into the countryside. This would be my hard work, perhaps life's work, and in it I would find the sort of satisfaction that I saw in Fiorina.

As I filled notebook after notebook with descriptions and sketches of Nature, I grew alarmed at the limitlessness and hardiness of my subject. One day, sitting in a field not far from the hazelnut grove, I was seized by the realization that it was I who was decomposing, not Nature, and that Nature was not only the cause of my decay but would be there to remove happily my remains once I was dead. The notebooks were a detailed description of my assassin.

I needed to talk to Sheila.

I found her in the studio of the house but could only see her feet. The rest was encased in live bees.

"We need to leave," I shouted into the bees.

Sheila painted by mixing pigments into unfiltered

beeswax. When heated, the wax drew bees. She worked with thousands of bees around her. They dove headfirst into her paintings, their little, soon-to-be-dead bodies wiggling in the wax.

Sheila was too far gone to appreciate the problem.

"The Borgo."

The words erupted from the bees. She was not too far gone.

The Borgo di Sutri was a hotel on the outskirts of town. It was there that I would escape from my predicament with Nature.

I left for the Borgo that evening.

The public rooms of the hotel were of the nicest sort—Oriental rugs, dark wood beams, leather chairs, chandeliers, newspapers neatly placed on every table. Everything was spacious. The dining room alone was large enough to hold hundreds of people.

That I was now in a hotel was hardly surprising. After leaving Nebraska, my pattern had been pretty much the same: selecting one city after another that I believed would provide a happy place to spend my life, I would check into a hotel and begin an energetic search for a spot to take root. After a few weeks, my enthusiasm would plunge; and the short stays in the hotels turned into years.

Since moving to New York I have lived in two of them:

one on Park Avenue and the other on 23rd Street. The hotel on Park Avenue had a crowd who gathered in the lounge late every evening to drink. Some, who had started drinking elsewhere, would do everything possible to meet up at the lounge. It was not uncommon to see them— drunk, dressed in dinner jackets—enter the bar on their hands and knees.

As for the hotel on 23rd Street, it too had a history of sotters, though of a more bohemian sort. A friend told me that when her mother passed away, she organized a dinner at the Spanish restaurant next to the lobby. The mother had lived in the hotel for decades and had been friends with the artists and poets who lived in the hotel. With a portion of the mother's ashes in the center of the table, each guest stood and delivered a eulogy. Toward the very end of the evening, one of the guests, a well-known poet, stood. He was, in addition to being one of her mother's best friends, the object of her mother's long but unsatisfied sexual interest. As everyone waited, he sprinkled her ashes over the top of the sangria and then downed the pitcher. With that, he sat back down.

Sheila had no difficulty with my affection for hotels.

Since she was an adolescent, she has traveled, often for years at a time, to the most obscure parts of the world, gathering images for her paintings. The places of interest to her rarely see visitors—mountains in central Asia, African villages, nomadic encampments in the Sahara and Middle East. Despite my attraction to her, nothing could move me to visit such places.

Knowing this, Sheila would find the nearest large city, locate a comfortable hotel, and make arrangements for a room to be fixed up in a way that as closely as possible resembled the one in which I was living. The staff were instructed to refer to me by my name and to do nothing that would suggest that I was somewhere other than my own hotel.

I was by no means the first of my relatives to live in a hotel.

There was a long tradition of it on both my father's and mother's sides. One of my great-uncles, having to leave Chicago because of his involvement in a local scandal, moved into a downtown hotel, where he lived anonymously for the rest of his life. When he needed money, he would step outside of the hotel and draw the first affluent person who passed by into a wager on whether my great-uncle could throw a pumpkin over the hotel's roof. The bet was atractive: the hotel was twelve stories high and my great-uncle a weak man. Even in his youth, he was a weak man.

The wager would end when my great-uncle took the

elevator to the top of a neighboring building and, pulling a baby pumpkin from his pocket, tossed it easily over the hotel. He would then return to the hotel with his winnings.

Whether my relatives were frightened by the size of large cities or their histories or their cultures, hotels allowed these men the illusion, if not the reality, of detachment from their surroundings and at the same time presented them with a small community of people (the permanent residents of the hotel) who shared their fears. And now I was running from another form of the never-changing—Nature.

My first night at the Borgo, I decided to have dinner in the dining room. I was welcomed there by a young woman, who, when I asked for a table, excused herself and searched the room. Returning, she reported to me that "no tables were available."

In the entire room, I saw not a single diner.

Surveying the void, it struck me that since arriving at the hotel I'd seen no other guests. More disturbing, I'd seen no bellmen or cleaning staff.

The hostess must have detected my concern, because she took my arm and led me to a seat in the lobby. "Wait here and you will see him."

As I sat there reading the newspaper, the hostess took

phone calls. To all callers she explained that the restaurant could not possibly take them and that it would be preferable if they didn't phone again.

None of this bothered me. I happened to know that there was at least one other person in the hotel and that he would soon be arriving. A possible dinner companion. The sort of shallow, worldly type of whom I was so fond.

At almost twelve o'clock, he arrived—a tiny old priest dressed in a floor-length black cassock. He had replaced the clasps on the back and sleeves of his cassock with enormous pearl buttons. Around his shoulders was a thick black cape and on his head a bulbous, three-cornered hat, pulled very near his eyebrows.

The priest moved slowly through the lobby of the Borgo—his skeleton squealing under the weight of his garments. Not having time to get from my seat, I bowed my head.

Looking up, I was staring into a milky thickness of a woman's thigh. The woman, wearing a short black skirt, emerald jewelry, and sunglasses, was just behind the priest. She motioned for me to follow.

The three of us, in tandem, walked through the lobby, passed the reception area, and headed out the front door of the hotel. I closed the door behind me.

The priest led us through the vacant parking lot in

front of the hotel. Halfway through the lot our destination emerged. Ahead, at the edge of the lot, was a fully lit but empty Renaissance chapel.

Once inside, the priest went to the front of the chapel. The woman took a seat in one of the pews. I sat behind her.

Facing the cross, the priest appeared to be challenging Christ, as if to say, "Okay, you've been talking about coming back, well this is the time." Seeing no response, the priest grew immediately contrite. He bowed his head and began to pray. As he did so, he grabbed the feet of Christ. Before long his fingertips began to move back and forth across the bottom of Christ's feet, and when the priest felt it safe to do so, he would glance up at Christ's face, checking for the reaction.

I got up from the pew. Having come to the Borgo to escape the enormity of Nature, I was not about to sit around while the little priest tickled the King to earth.

I learned later that the priest's name was Don Augusto. A brilliant man, he had been kept on at his church until he was suspected of being too disturbed to continue his duties. From time to time he would arrive in the piazza in a three-wheeled, one-person vehicle that was stuffed with dogs and the smoke of the two or three cigarettes he puffed simultaneously. Attired in the antique wardrobe of a priest, he was known throughout town for rarely bathing.

Back at the hotel, I found the front door locked. No amount of pounding retrieved anyone from inside.

Noticing a window open on the second floor of the hotel, I climbed the stone wall and entered.

Unlocking the door to my room, I knew what awaited me. As soon as I lay on my bed, my mind was cleaved open to the reality of my own death. All thought was overthrown, replaced by the emotions of imminent and unending emptiness. I was experiencing my own oblivion.

The malignancy of the vision was blunted, finally, by its familiarity, for so often have I encountered it, for so many years has it been with me, that I've come to appreciate, perhaps even enjoy, what it has revealed—the enormousness of Death, its vacant strength and its lush clarity. Death has, in short, engaged me as little else. For most, I suspect, the knowledge of death is pushed off, delayed until they are too old and exhausted to enjoy it. If youth is wasted on the young, death is wasted on the old. That said, I would rather not be so taken by visions of death, but it is not something that I entirely control, and on that day, my encounter with death was set off by

Nature and made unstoppable by the sight of a once brilliant man standing deranged before the cross.

The next morning, I returned home.

It was my good luck that within two weeks, the artist whose house we were renting, a woman by the name of Michele Zalopany, moved back to Sutri. Her return required that we find a new place to live, less mired in Nature.

The new place was situated on the north end of town, high above vegetative intrusions. Those few birds that had the talent to reach the house were so exhausted by the flight that they were no match for me.

The house was not far from the road leading to Rome. On the road were a car wash and a café. Other cafés are more comfortable, all have more congenial proprietors, but none serves a better espresso. The locals attribute this to the Illy coffee, one of the finest in Italy, which is served by the café, and the café is referred to by some as the "Illy caffè."

Many people come to the Illy café. For those who linger, there is a television set and a video game machine. Those interested in neither television nor video games may amuse themselves in front of a large glass case filled with miniature red cars. I suspect the collection is special, because people come into the café just to look at the cars.

Other customers sit on the terrace and watch the car wash and on a hot day cool off in its mist. I sit on the terrace.

One cold morning, I was inside the café. At the table next to me was a man whom I had not seen before. He was staring into a paper bag. I'm sure that he had noticed me looking at him, for he reached into the bag, took out an object, and asked me if I recognized it. A Danish with the center scooped out and replaced with custard—it was a pastry served in every café in Sutri. Sheila is fond of them.

"The name?"

He was testing me.

I shook my head.

"The Radetzky," he announced, the words bent with irony—the irony being that this pastry, so popular throughout the region, was named after an Austrian field marshal, Count Joseph Radetzky, who spent much of his long life killing Italians. For the better part of twenty-five years, Radetzky ruled over the Lombardy-Venetian territory, and at the age of eighty-three orchestrated the defeat of the Piedmontese army, as led by Charles Albert, King of Sardinia-Piedmont.

A resident of the town who has been known to eat two

or three Radetzkys a day later commented that it was named Radetzky because it was the only way that "the Italians could get their teeth into him." But Radetzky, as the man in the Illy café pointed out, was not the first nor last military leader to have his name attached to a food.

"Caesar salad, Beef Wellington, the Napoleon, the Bismarck. . ."

Colonel Sanders, I thought.

"You're American?" he asked.

"Yes."

"You eat pancakes?"

"Yes."

"No one feels good after eating pancakes."

He was right: no matter how good or bad they are, no matter how thick or thin, how few or how many you eat, no one feels good after eating pancakes. This man was a philosopher of the mundane, blessed with deep insight into subjects of no significance.

The Philosopher was also responsible for the observation that as good as the restaurants are in town, the Sutrini rarely eat in them. The reason for this, he maintained, is that the women in Sutri believe that their meals are superior to those prepared in restaurants—not just the restaurants in Sutri, but all restaurants. Men, when eating out, are forced to condemn perfectly good meals lest they offend their wives.

But the Philosopher noted an important qualification to his own rule: pizza. The women in Sutri are happy to eat pizza in restaurants. Despite having their own, often quite sophisticated, pizza ovens and despite the fact that the women of Sutri are able to turn out superb pizza, they feel that their pizzas fall short of the pizza in the local restaurants.

Most Americans dismiss Italian pizza with the observation that pizza was invented in the United States. My experience is that American and Italian pizza are different foods: American pizza is stewy, complex, and flaccid; Italian pizza, fresh, simple, and rigid.

The difference is the tomatoes. The tomatoes used in American sauces are by and large tasteless. American chefs, forced to compensate for a bland sauce, add more ingredients than the crust can possibly bear. Italians don't have this problem. Their tomatoes, recently from the vine and of much higher quality, produce a tomato sauce that needs little else to make it an excellent topping.

The best pizza in Sutri is served at two restaurants: Ladrone and Fontenelle. Both have similar atmospheres:

large, boisterous, and impossible to get into after nine in the evening. Wine is abandoned in favor of beer. Children sit politely at great tables of relatives. The kitchens are open to view as women, wielding long pallets, slide pizzas in and out of the ovens. As for the pizzas, the tomato sauces are simple and fragrant, the crusts delicate, almost inconsequential.

My few discussions with the Philosopher lasted hours, and while I would like to say they resulted in a friendship or even a fondness for each other I would be misstating it. The Philosopher could not contain his contempt for questions that reflected clumsy thinking or that ranged beyond the trivial.

When I related the story about Angela demanding to know if Frank was a man or woman, the Philosopher looked me in the face and said: "My life is swollen with fools."

The problem was not with the story. The Philosopher had no interest in the story, other than to point out that the Hebrews of antiquity had used the word "feet" as a metaphor for genitals and that this would explain Frank's interest in shoes—articles that hide the feet. Where I had fallen down was in my description of Angela as a cherub. Cherubs, the Philosopher corrected me, citing Ezekiel, have the body of a man and the face of an animal or bird, with four wings and human hands underneath the wings. The soles of their feet are the hooves of calves. Their bodies are covered in eyes.

"Eyes?"

"Did your Angela look like that?" he shouted.

If this was unpleasant, it was nothing compared with the exchange we had over tomato juice.

The episode began when I brought an orange juice back to the table. As I sat down, the Philosopher yelled out from across the room:

"Do you ever drink tomato juice?"

"No. I never drink tomato juice."

"You drink it on airplanes."

There was no way that he could have known this. I do drink tomato juice on airplanes. On airplanes I only drink tomato juice. I complimented him on his insight.

"You flatter me because you are weak."

True.

But he was not done.

"Do you have any idea why people who hate tomato juice drink it on airplanes?"

After being accused of weakness, I was not about to back down. I spent days thinking through the question, discussing it with Sheila and others. Each time we came up with something, I would bring it down to the Philosopher. I suggested, to take one example, that the drinking of a blood-red juice was a vestige of the ritual in which animals were slaughtered so as to ward off future trouble.

My efforts only saddened him. His condescension was finally too much: one evening I challenged him to give me the answer to his own question. When he refused, I left the café, accusing him of not knowing the answer.

Once outside I looked back at him. His body was framed by little red cars, drops of frozen blood, and nothing he could do, no power of his imagination, could thaw them.

I regret my decision to leave the café that day. When I saw him again, he was not the same. There were no more discussions, no more shouting.

If I had one small consolation, it was that he did give me the answer as to why people drink tomato juice on airplanes.

The Philosopher's explanation went something like this: The indefinite status of the tomato (fruit or vegetable) makes it the perfect food for the traveler, who is, himself, in an indefinite or ambiguous state—separated from the place of departure but not yet attached to the place of arrival. As plane travel (versus slower means of transportation) presents an intensified experience of indefinite identity, tomato juice is the concentrated form of the symbol of uncertain identity, the tomato.

The last time I saw the Philosopher he was wandering outside the Illy café. He seemed disoriented. I asked him where he had been.

"The slough."

A reference, perhaps, to the Slough of Despond. I asked him whether he would walk with me to the top of the hill and have a coffee in the piazza. He declined.

There is an estate that sits at the edge of Sutri. It is owned by Piperno, a Jew, who, the Sutrini tell me, made a great deal of money in Rome and with it bought a vast piece of land outside of Sutri. On the greater part of that land Piperno built a villa with formal gardens, a tennis court, and a tall fence. Piperno divided the remainder of the property into smaller plots of land, which were then sold.

Walking by the Piperno estate, I never saw anyone at home. People in the town say that Piperno is old and only uses the house on weekends or during the summers. But everyone agrees that Piperno is there. Despite this, no one knows what he looks like.

The possibility that the Philosopher was Piperno made a great deal of sense: it would explain why people knew him to be around but had never met him. It would also explain his references to the Hebrews.

But when I thought back to my few encounters with the Philosopher, I recalled that each time he left the café, he left on foot, and that when he left, he always headed west. That was not the direction of the bus stop, or even the direction of Piperno's estate. It was the direction of the former convent of Saint Paul—now an abandoned assemblage of bricks and stone, overgrown with grass and trees.

No one would live there, except someone too poor to have a home or too deranged to want one. That person might, when it was cold outside, come down to the Illy café, find a piece of food left on a table, and consume it carefully, making certain that it lasted for the rest of the day. And that, presumably, would allow him plenty of time for reflection.

But on my walks around the ruins, I never saw the Philosopher, and no one ever mentioned that there was a man living in the ruins. When the Philosopher had not shown up at the café for a month or two, I began asking around. But no one had seen him. Even the people at the bar had difficulty recalling him.

I had trouble forgetting him. He had succeeded where I had failed: he had created a clearing—a place beyond the reach of the powers that threatened him. Not only had he kept Nature and history and culture at bay (freeing himself from the burden of their logic, categories, and false assumptions), but he had also, through the quick muscle of his imagination, beaten back the smallest creatures—the clutter of the quotidian—that normally escape notice but are no less dangerous. He saw absolutely everything around him, picked up those objects that were the most ordinary, and, rubbing them together, created light. On the day he is found frozen in a field, or dead in a plush bed, his body will be covered in eyes.

Luciano's New Home

IF Luciano De Marco is sitting in the square, be assured he is involved in a discourse on Italian politics or history. There is virtually no subject within these fields about which he does not have a definite and well-thought-out opinion. There are some who consider Luciano arrogant; but there is no one who challenges the depth of his knowledge.

It was not always so. Before moving to Sutri, Luciano passed out peanuts on airplanes.

For the thirty years that he spent as an airline attendant, Luciano believed he was happy. Then one morning he woke up, looked at his wife, and said, "Maria-Christina, I'm not pushing the cart today."

After quitting his job, he saw no need to live in Rome: the streets were crowded, real estate prices were rising, and crime was up. He began looking for another place to live.

Other flight attendants told him of Sutri. It was, they said, a quiet and beautiful place. It was also a place from which Maria-Christina could commute to her job in Rome. So Luciano De Marco and Maria-Christina moved to Sutri.

It did not take Luciano long to discover that his fellow attendants were right. During his first summer in Sutri, when the heat made Rome unbearable, Sutri, at the top of a hill, was full of strong breezes. Moreover, Luciano loved the Piazza del Comune, spending much of his time sitting in the sun, reading the sports pages. As he approached fifty and wanting a family, Luciano decided to buy a piece of property and build a house.

The land Luciano bought was at the top of a hill overlooking Sutri. When the designs for the house were complete and all the forms filled out, Luciano waited for the town to approve his plan. While he waited he sat in the square talking to friends.

Six months passed; then a year. His frustration grew.

He began to study the laws of the town.

Two years went by. His reading shifted from local ordinances to national law and from national law to natural law, and from there, to political theory, and finally to philosophy. Books filled his house.

More than one person has advised him that acceptance of his plans awaited one simple step: a payment to the appropriate public official.

But Luciano refused to pay the bribe. Through his extensive reading he had become convinced that the only way the political system could be fixed was through individual acts of resistance.

Nearly seven years have gone by and Luciano has yet to receive approval for his plans. Luciano, in fact, has not even been notified that the city has received his plans. Luciano is locked in a terrible and solitary struggle.

When Luciano is not in the square, he is home preparing meals for Maria-Christina. The construction of his house delayed, he has had time to perfect his skills as a cook.

Luciano's best dish is pasta with garlic and oil. The recipe could not be simpler: boil pasta (any will do); while the pasta is cooking, heat two tablespoons of olive oil; sauté one clove of smashed garlic and a whole chili pepper in the heated oil; throw out the garlic and pepper; when the pasta is ready, drain and stir the pasta into the pan of oil; transfer the pasta to a bowl and mix in half a cup of grated Pecorino Romano; just prior to serving, pour raw olive oil over the top.

Lately, Luciano has begun to refine his political theories.

For months he applied his intelligence to the development of a distinction between *controllo* (control) and *dominio* (domination). The metaphor that he finally hit upon to illustrate the difference came to him one evening when he was making dinner. "If a man places his hands around the neck of the rabbit," Luciano explained to me, "he controls the rabbit; if the same man inserts his fingers into the rectum of the rabbit, he dominates the rabbit." After people in the town indicated that they did not entirely understand the metaphor, Luciano changed the rabbit to a chicken.

Concerned that his prolonged fight with the city has begun to affect him, I suggested that he leave Sutri. Luciano would not hear of it.

Every Sunday, Luciano drives out to visit his land. One Sunday Luciano and I made the trip. The land was covered in a sheet of long grass, and just beneath the top of the grass were wild mushrooms. At the end of the land is a grove of cherry trees.

As we walked his land, picking mushrooms and cherries, I asked about the future. He told me that if he still hadn't heard from the city by the end of the year, he would file a legal action to force the city to make a decision on his application—a suit that could bankrupt his family.

I asked him what he would do with the land if the city denied him the right to build his house?

Looking out from his property toward Sutri, Luciano answered, "Raise chickens."

Pontius Pilate

F this Luciano is certain: if he were from Sutri instead of Rome, his house would have been approved immediately, with no bribe.

Luciano's difficulties, he and others believe, are symptomatic of a society that is impenetrable, largely irrational, and openly hostile to anyone who is not Sutrini. If you are to believe the outsiders, the Sutrini discriminate against them in commercial transactions, refuse them admission to religious societies, prevent them from purchasing the most desirable real estate, and make them the subject of insufferable accusations in the form of gossip. "A festival of humiliation," as one outsider put it.

The resistance of Sutrini to outsiders is well known

and neatly memorialized in the saying (repeated by Sutrini and outsider alike) "If you live in Sutri for a hundred years, you won't have a friend; if you live in Sutri for five hundred years, you'll have a friend, but you'll regret it."

All of this is infuriating to the Romans, who constitute the majority of the outsiders and are, with few exceptions, wealthier, better educated, and more sophisticated than the Sutrini. They live in nicer houses, drive better cars, send their children to private schools, and from this feel entitled to refer to the Sutrini as *contadini*—peasants.

And yet the peasants have inverted the hierarchy, keeping the outsiders in an ever inferior station by a continuous stream of insults, large and small, overt and subtle. When we first arrived in town, an old woman motioned Sheila over to her bench in the Piazza del Comune.

She had a secret to tell Sheila. Sheila bent down.

"Remove my shoes and rub my feet," she whispered.

Sensing that Sheila might have some objection to this, the old woman said, with some understanding, "Okay, rub my back."

When Sheila continued to hesitate but with her ear still near the woman's mouth, the woman whispered random phrases in German.

The conflict between Romans and Sutrini has resulted

in a bifurcation of the town: one rarely sees Sutrini in conversation with non-Sutrini. Their children don't mix, never intermarry, and if someone passes by a table of Sutrini in the square, the first thing that is said after the person passes is "Sutri" (with approving nods) or "outsider" (usually accompanied by a shake of the head). Sutri/outsider is the first and most elemental classification of humans in Sutri.

There are a number of theories that explain the Sutrini personality. By far the most widely held is that the Sutrini are descended from the Etruscans and thereby embody an ancient and unpleasant collection of traits that is found nowhere else in Italy.

"People from Sutri," a man explained to me one day, "are the last remnants of Etruria, and the Etruscans were an insular, self-protective, and two-faced people. From their ancestors, Sutrini know how to get along with people, make them feel comfortable, and then plot against them, doing everything possible to advance the interest of their fellow Sutrini over you."

While this theory of the Etruscan personality is compelling, there is this one detail: Romans ran the Etruscans out of Sutri five centuries before the birth of Christ and as far as anybody can tell, they haven't been back since. It is even possible that the Sutrini were never

Etruscan. The Falisci—a tribe of Sabine derivation—lived just to the east of Sutri (in the area of Civita Castellana) and may have been the town's original inhabitants.

It could easily be concluded that the Sutrini, convinced that they are Etruscan, are suffering from a mass delusion.

At almost any time of day a tall, strikingly thin man with a half-grown beard can be found sitting alone in the square. His name is Paolo Gnecco.

Paolo is the last person that anyone in the town would expect to have an opinion on the Sutrini. Asked his opinion on any subject, Paolo will comment that he is nothing more than a part-time translator and that his opinions could be of interest to no one. In this he is undoubtedly sincere.

What Paolo does not tell people is that before moving to town he was a social anthropologist, trained at the University of Chicago. Having lived and worked through-out the world, Paolo speaks and writes flawless English, Spanish, and French. He reads German, but claims, probably falsely, not to speak it. In all languages, he is clear and intelligent.

When I was finally able to persuade Paolo to talk to me about Sutri, he began his analysis by drawing an analogy to Mexicans, who, according to Paolo, prefer to identify with tribes remote in time and culture rather than with the Spaniards. Similarly, the Sutrini cannot bear the idea of being associated with the Romans, who colonized Sutri in antiquity. During this time, the Romans not only forced the Sutrini to pay money to Rome but also emptied the graves in which the Sutrini buried their dead. ("Even our dead weren't safe," remarked one local.)

In recent years, Paolo pointed out, Romans have begun to move out of Rome and into the countryside, with Sutri the most beautiful village within commuting distance of Rome. At the same time that Romans have started moving to Sutri, the Sutrini have begun to leave. The reason for this, Paolo said, is that the Sutrini are becoming increasingly dependent on jobs located in larger towns in the region (Ronciglione and Viterbo). A recent plague among the hazelnut trees has accelerated this trend.

The simultaneous influx of Romans and the constriction of the local economy have made the Sutrini extremely anxious. The people of Sutri have begun to romanticize their past because they sense that their society is dying.

In reworking their past, the Sutrini have latched onto Ciro Nispi-Landi. In the nineteenth century, Nispi-Landi published a massive book on Sutri. In it, he argued strenuously, if not convincingly, that the Sutrini were and continue to be Etruscans. Paolo observed that Nispi-Landi, himself an outsider, married a Sutrini. Paolo believed that Nispi-Landi wrote his history as a way of winning his way into Sutri society.

Evidence that the Sutrini are involved in a program of myth creation is found in the person of Romolo. He is in his late seventies, articulate, a member in high standing of the church, a cousin of Gino Guidi, and for the Sutrini, the definitive authority on the history of the town. Romolo has read and collected virtually everything written on Sutri and has even distributed his own critiques of the works of other historians.

Romolo, who heard from one of the regulars at the Guidi Caffè that I was having a pair of boots made, asked whether I was aware that the boot itself was invented by a Sutrini. When I told him that I knew nothing about this, he recounted the following story:

Julius Caesar, having decided to attack Gaul, determined that the shoes that his soldiers were wearing would be inadequate for the campaign. This led Caesar to announce a competition in which all the great cobblers in Italy were asked to submit a shoe. A cobbler from Sutri created the boot and sent it to Caesar. When Caesar saw the boot, he held it up over his head and proclaimed *"isti valent"* (they are good), which over time contracted into *"stivali"* (boots).

When Romolo was done with the story, I jokingly asked whether he had made it up. "No," he said regretfully, "but I'll tell you one I did."

Romolo then recounted that at a time when other Italian towns were holding festivals celebrating local foods, certain citizens of Sutri thought it would be a good idea to have a festival for the fagioli regina. The city government was too lethargic to do anything about it, and Sutri remained without a festival. The citizens approached Romolo with the problem, and Romolo, after reflecting on it, came up with this solution: the bean advocates needed a story that elevated the fagioli regina of Sutri to a position of such historical significance that the city would be forced to declare a bean festival.

When the citizens told Romolo that they did not have such a story, Romolo told them not to be concerned; he would create one. This is what Romolo gave them:

Charlemagne suffered from terrible gout. His gout was so bad that his advisers feared that the pain would interfere with his efforts to unify Europe. One of Charlemagne's advisers, whose name has been lost, had heard of the curative power of the fagioli regina from Sutri and recommended a visit to the town. Charlemagne left immediately for Sutri, where he spent a week eating only beans. At the end of the week he was cured.

Romolo's story was so appealing it spread throughout the town, throughout the region, and even made its way into historical journals and guides to Italy. The force of the story, as Romolo had predicted, caused the government of Sutri to institute an annual bean festival.

The real beauty of the story, Romolo observed, is that the fagioli regina of Sutri were native to the Americas and thus not introduced to Europe until long after Charlemagne's death. When I asked Romolo whether this deception troubled him, he responded, "If the purpose of history is to make people feel better, why not make it good?"

Even Romolo, I guessed, had his limits. He did not, I ventured, believe the legend that Sutri was founded by Saturn. "No," he assured me, "it goes back before that."

"How far?"

Romolo's head sank slowly backward; and as it did, his eyelids slid shut at the same velocity that his head was moving in the opposite direction. From below the table his arm rose until it came to a halt near his ear.

He began to wave his fingers, brushing away the present.

He was very far back—beyond the Romans, the Etruscans. He was still waving. Then he stopped.

An ecstatic look claimed his face.

Eden. Sutri was there from the beginning: a place that existed before time and now waited for time to exhaust itself.

At that instant, Romolo became indistinguishable from my relatives.

When my ancestors arrived in Omaha, it was a frontier town and Nebraska not yet a state. They remained in the town through the twentieth century and now into the twenty-first. My grandparents, parents, myself, and all of my brothers went to the same high school in downtown Omaha, overlooking the Missouri River. As cynical as they may have become about all other aspects of their lives, I've not heard a negative word about Nebraska.

Before I left Omaha for college, my grandmother's brother, who lived in Omaha all of his life, asked me if I'd come see him. When I arrived, he told me that he was sick. I think he sensed it would be the last time we saw one another. I was very fond of him.

He had often given me advice, and now I expected him to offer words that would assist me as I went out into the world. Instead he told me a story.

When Omaha was quite young, he and a group of his friends played cards every afternoon at a bar near the river. One day the Black Jew, a regular at the bar, came in and ordered what he always ordered—a boilermaker. On that day, the bartender, One-Eye Peroni, refused to serve the Black Jew.

The Black Jew repeated the request and again One-Eye refused. This time the Black Jew caught One-Eye glancing toward the corner of the bar. There in the corner was the new owner of the bar, sitting with his associates.

The owner was a serious gentleman who had gone East to school and since his return had spent a fair amount of his time thinking of ways to draw more outsiders to the city. He and his partners had plans and had bought up property around town.

The Black Jew understood that One-Eye was just following instructions and was good enough to leave the bar without causing trouble.

An hour later the Black Jew returned. He ordered a drink. One-Eye said no, and the Black Jew left.

On his way out, he stuck a knife into the owner's forehead.

The Black Jew was apprehended (since there were few others in town who answered to that name). The Black Jew confessed, and sentencing was set for the following week. Nebraska was hanging people back then, and this would surely be the Black Jew's fate.

A week passed and my great-uncle and his friends were at the card table. The sentencing was scheduled for that afternoon and someone mentioned the Black Jew. A conversation followed and my great-uncle was sent over to speak with the judge.

When the judge came out on the bench, there was a large crowd, including all of the associates of the deceased and some of his family. There was a lot of excitement in the court, so the judge had to pound a few times to make sure everyone was paying attention.

With quiet restored, the judge recited something in Latin and then announced the sentence: "The Black Jew goes free."

My great-uncle went back to the bar. The Black Jew arrived a few minutes later, and the judge shortly thereafter. One-Eye had a boilermaker ready.

I'd heard the story before, many times, and must admit to a certain disappointment at hearing it again.

As I left my great-uncle, it struck me that I'd never asked about the Latin.

My great-uncle smiled. I was slightly less stupid than he'd imagined.

"*Quis separabit?*"*

On the south side of the Piazza Cavour is a café. The café and the somewhat dilapidated building in which it is housed attract no attention. But if one looks carefully there is something on the façade of the building, which appears on no other building of the town: the crest of the Doria-Pamphili family, one of the most important families in Italy.

Today the building is occupied by Peter Hunt and his wife, Ornella. They are a handsome and smart couple who years ago moved into the palazzo and have devoted themselves to its restoration. They believe that in addition to the Doria-Pamphilis, the palazzo was once the residence of Cardinal Manosio. Most recently, the palazzo belonged to the Mezzadonnas.

I met Peter through Paolo. Like Paolo, Peter is a translator. Unlike Paolo, who resides at the Guidi, Peter takes his coffee and Radetzky at the café at the west end of the square, next to Lello's panties. It was there that we sat and discussed Sutri.

* "Who shall separate us?"

Extrapolating on Paolo's thoughts, Peter observed that the recent influx of outsiders into Sutri stirs an animosity dating back to the days when Sutri was part of the papal state. Those who sought to challenge the power of the pope would capture Sutri, and the pope, given the strategic importance of the town (the last fortified city before Rome) and its religious significance (the first papal territory), would be forced to retake it. Sutri was constantly being conquered and reconquered, and consequently the Sutrini developed the ability to tolerate everyone but liked and trusted no one—unless, of course, they were undeniably Sutrini, which meant they were from a family that had lived in Sutri for generations, had married into a similar family, and had shown nothing but unfaltering loyalty to the town.

The evening before my conversation with Peter, I had dined with Bruce Johnston. Because he had been reporting on Italy for years and had lived in a number of cities, including Sutri, I asked Bruce whether the Sutrini were different from the other Italians he had met.

"Of course," he said without pausing, "they're mad."

When I repeated this to Peter, he nodded his head in recognition and uttered two words that I had heard countless times since I'd come to town:

"Pontius Pilate."

When the Romans in Sutri are feeling especially irritated with the Sutrini or are just in a bad mood, they will announce—usually under the pretext of providing visitors with helpful information about the town and usually in a café so as to be certain that as many Sutrini as possible overhear it—that Pontius Pilate was born and raised in Sutri. They don't really have to say more; the message is clear—it was Sutri that bred Pontius Pilate and instilled in him that potent mixture of paganism and bitter temperament that allowed him to execute the Lord. In short, the Sutrini killed Jesus.

Of all the insults that are tossed back and forth between the Sutrini and the Romans, this is the most inflammatory.

The Sutrini, needless to say, have a different version of the story of Pontius Pilate.

Romolo once told me, with a certainty suggesting that he may have actually known Pilate, that "Pilate was born in Rome and sent to Sutri as a functionary of the state. There was nothing we liked about him and as soon as we could, we sent him back to Rome." When I asked Romolo where Pontius Pilate lived while he was in Sutri, Romolo gestured toward an area behind the Guidi Caffè. That area contains one of the most distinguished palazzos in Sutri, the Palazzo Mezzaroma.

I asked Romolo why, if the Sutrini so disliked Pontius Pilate, they would have allowed him to live in that palazzo.

Even the polite Romolo couldn't contain himself. He cried, "Pontius Pilate in the Palazzo Mezzaroma? Never! He lived in the parking lot in front of the palazzo—we never gave him a home; that shows you what we thought of him."

The whole discussion was so upsetting to Romolo that he was forced to take a stroll around the piazza. Returning to the table, a calmer Romolo posed this question: "If Pontius Pilate had been born in Sutri would Adrian IV have come here?"

The argument raised one of the historical events of which the Sutrini are proudest: the meeting in the twelfth century between Pope Adrian IV and Frederick Barbarossa—a meeting held for the purpose of discussing the coronation of Barbarossa as Holy Roman Emperor. This meeting is reviewed in great detail in Nispi-Landi's treatise on Sutri.

Over dinner at Il Buco with one of the Romans, I happened to mention the meeting in Sutri of Adrian IV and Barbarossa. The Roman scoffed.

"You have obviously been taken in by a Sutrini—the pope and Barbarossa never met in Sutri."

"How could that be? Nispi-Landi says so."

"Nispi-Landi an authority? Nispi-Landi…" He began to laugh and then laughed so hard he choked. Salvatore, the owner, glanced over at the table, hoping for the worst.

Dislodging goat from his throat, the Roman continued: "Nispi-Landi is an apologist for the Sutrini. Totally untrustworthy. Nispi-Landi believes that Sutri was founded by Saturn."

The Roman was right. Nispi-Landi says that Sutri (along with a city in Japan) was founded by the Roman god.

Claiming that he had something that would set me straight, the Roman left the restaurant. Back minutes later, he had an armful of leather-bound volumes. These turned out to be nothing less than Ferdinand Gregorovius's *History of the City of Rome in the Middle Ages*.

"Here," said the Roman, pointing to a passage in which Gregorovius states that the German army was encamped at "Campo Grasso," which was not in Sutri but "near Sutri," when the pope rode to the royal tent to greet Barbarossa.

The next day I sought out Romolo to confront him with Gregorovius's version of the meeting. I found him sitting with a friend at the Guidi. Romolo didn't even bother looking down at the text. He raised his hand from the table, flattened his hand palm side down, and moved

it back and forth under his chin—a gesture roughly translated as "Get this away from me, it's ridiculous."

Romolo's friend spat, "Dilettante. Gregorovius was not
Italian, had no training, no university position."

The man's face was turning red. I removed the book
from the table.

He grabbed it back.

"Look at this!" He was pointing to a passage in which
the great German historian describes Jerusalem as the cap-
ital of the "small and impotent Jewish race."

"If he did that to the Jews," the man concluded, "what
do you think he did to us?"

The strangeness of the debate over whether the pope
and Barbarossa met in Sutri—indeed the oddity of almost
all of the great moments in Sutri's history—is that the
event was, from all accounts, an embarrassment that
few cities would wish to recall. Sutri was selected only
because it was convenient: Adrian IV, originally Nicholas
Beakspear (the only Englishman to be pope), was so
despised in Rome that he had taken up residence in Civita
Castellana (not far from Sutri); with Adrian in Civita
Castellana and Barbarossa coming from the north, Sutri
was the logical place for the two to meet.

Whether one believes that the meeting took place in or

near Sutri, what followed in June of 1155 is undisputed: As the pope, on horse, approached Barbarossa, he expected Barbarossa to come forward and hold the papal stirrups—an indignity endured, or so says Gregorovius, by many medieval princes. But the German king would have none of it and refused to get up out of his chair. The cardinals accompanying the pope sensed bloodshed and fled. The pope remained.

What followed was a detailed and lengthy negotiation between Barbarossa and the pope over the holding of the papal stirrup—a discussion that carried on into the next day, when the ritual was repeated and Barbarossa finally took the stirrup. In Nispi-Landi's version, the pope actually stepped on the head of Barbarossa. No one, historians included, seems to remember anything about the meeting of these two potentates other than the story of the stirrup.

Peter Hunt believes that the Sutrini have been warped by the thought that they, a community of such piety, should be associated with, if not responsible for, Pilate. For the Sutrini, Pilate is a historical hernia, bulging into places that it did not belong, namely the present.

"The people of Sutri," Peter warned, "must come to grips with the idea of Pilate. It would help, for example, if they were able to see him in a positive light."

Peter set down his Radetzky.

"If it were not for Pilate, there might have been no Christianity; and if there was no Christianity, Western civilization might have taken a more horrible turn than it actually did. Pilate got the ball rolling." Peter stopped. He leaned back suddenly and stared upward; his face began to twist. He was undoubtedly viewing the course of history without Pilate. Then again it may have been the Radetzky.

The one person who seems to have been left out of the debate over Pontius Pilate is the director of the Museum of Sutri, the keeper of the documents that place Pontius Pilate in the town. This may be because when asked about the record on Pilate's stay in Sutri, he claims to have little to say.

But there is no modesty here: the director says that the only evidence of Pontius Pilate's being in Sutri is a marble tablet on which are carved the names "L. Pontius" and "L. Pontius Aquila." Since *pontius* was an official title, the marble stands as no evidence at all.

It was hard for me to believe that the never-ending controversy over Pontius Pilate, with its accompanying insults and hurt feelings, was based on nothing. I drove into Rome to track down what people say is the definitive book on Pontius Pilate. Searching through it, I found no reference to Sutri. The author must have made a mistake.

Entering the Plaza Hotel, I found a phone, intending to

call the author in London. As I raised the receiver, I imagined the conversation.

"Excuse me, are you aware that Pilate lived in Sutri?"

"Where?"

"Probably in the parking lot. In front of the Mezzaromas; in back of the Mezzadonnas."

"Who is this?"

I returned the receiver to the phone.

Not far from the car wash and Illy café, just beneath the cliff on the south side of town, is a shack. Inside the shack is an accumulation of old and broken objects. These have been assembled by a woman named Marina and are for sale to the public.

I would often wander down to the shack to look for books, which, in keeping with the rest of items in the place, were mangled. Many, I imagined, had been left on the roadsides or pastures by pilgrims on their way to Rome. Many of the books were Bibles, and I found myself spending an increasing amount of time reading those pages of scripture that had not been made opaque by tire marks or food.

It was during one such reading, as I stood alone in

Marina's shop, that I discovered that Eden—the Paradise to which Romolo seemed to be gesturing in our conversation about the origins of Sutri—was quite different from the Eden that I learned of in childhood. Adam and Eve, whom I had been taught were amiable imbeciles, were actually possessed of a fine intelligence, including the capacity for reason and reflection. I would have read on but I was impeded by a small patch of animal that had been crushed into the text.

Despite this, I purchased the book and walked it down to the Illy. The Philosopher was in his chair.

Placing the text in front of him, I explained my observation. I waited while the Philosopher reviewed the passage. After a good amount of time, the Philosopher picked up a fork and wedged it into the animal. Tearing it from the Bible, he sniffed it.

"Fig."

The first food mentioned in the Bible. And this was a tiny miracle because there were, as far as I knew, no figs in Sutri.

The day was about over and I thought how it would be to see Sheila and our daughter. I wandered back up the hill to my house.

In the days that followed, I grew convinced that I'd

witnessed a transubstantiation—the beast had not stained the text, the text had made sweet the beast. In the back of my mind, there was the thought that this prefigured my own change.

The Boot Maker

WHILE the square is closed to cars, it is open to horses. One often encounters some- one riding a horse through the square to pick up groceries or visit a friend or simply show off their horse. The first time I saw this was when a young man, dressed entirely in white and wearing an ascot, came through the western gate of the city at full gallop, down a stone path and then into the square, where he made a stunning halt in front of the Guidis' bread shop and dis- mounted—all to pick up a small roll to be consumed with his morning coffee.

This rider belonged to a fraternal society devoted to horses. The society has a meeting place in the center of Sutri and at least once a year, it holds a feast set up on a forested hill just outside of town. Members of the society ride or drive their horses to the feast. The horses are tied to the trees surrounding the tables, and by the end of the afternoon the entire hillside is an ascending field of horses, buggies, trees, and crooked light dangling from the leaves.

The region's long-standing affection for horses has supported the finest boot makers in Italy. The boot makers construct two types of riding boots: a boot worn by those who ride an English saddle and a boot worn by the *butteri*, the cowboys of the region who round up cattle in the countryside. The boots of the *butteri* come to the knee and lace up the side through a series of interconnected strands of leather.

Shortly after I found a stable in which to ride (an interest left over from Nebraska), Enrico Guidi, the son of Enzo, told me that if I wanted a pair of boots, the greatest of all the boot makers was located nearby. Two days later, Enrico, Paolo, and I arrived at his shop.

The boot maker sat behind his bench in a tiny room filled in one corner with boots and in another with wooden molds, nails, rolls of leather, and glue. The boot maker had no assistants, no desk, no papers, just the bench where he cut and stitched boots.

After the introductions, I sat down next to the boot maker, removed my shoes, and readied myself for the extensive measurements I knew would be necessary.

I waited as the boot maker completed the tasks before him on his bench. I continued to wait. When I finally extended my foot toward him in the hope that he would begin the measurements, he looked at me in disgust.

I was a fool. This man did not need to take a single measurement: he needed only to look at my foot, absorbing the innumerable measurements with a glance of his eye. I had insulted him by presenting my foot. Ashamed, I slipped my shoe back on and left the shop. The boots, I was informed by Enrico, would be ready when the boot maker decided they were.

Two months went by before Enrico reported that I could pick up the boots. That afternoon I returned to the shop. As I entered the shop, I saw the boots on the workbench. They were magnificent.

So as not to insult the boot maker a second time, I picked up the boots and started to leave without trying them on.

But the boot maker stopped me. He gestured toward

the chair next to his bench. Whatever offense had been given in my previous encounter was now forgiven.

Taking a seat, I slipped on one of the boots.

I had felt nothing like it before. My foot was floating, as if no part of my foot were touching the boot. I caught the boot maker smiling. He gained pleasure from seeing the expression on his customers' faces when putting on his boots.

I too smiled, and as the two of us sat there smiling, not quite at each other but equally pleased, it came to me that the sensation of not having my foot touch the boot was because no part of my foot *was* touching the boot. The boot was at the very least six or seven sizes too large; my foot was not in a shoe, it was in a pasta pot.

Before I could say anything, the boot maker reached down and yanked off the boot. Staring at my foot, staring at the boot, staring at my foot again, the smile no longer on his face, he waved me out of the shop, instructing me to return the following week.

When I returned, the boots were once again propped on his bench. They were the same pair and again I was impressed with their beauty.

I no longer had to worry about the boots being too large for my feet. I knew this because the tops of the boots were so small I couldn't possibly have gotten my feet into them.

When I mentioned the problem to the boot maker, he motioned toward the shelves filled with other customers' boots.

"If you can find something that fits, take it."

Seeing no other solution, I started searching through the boots and soon found a pair that fit—even the color and leather, which I would not otherwise have chosen, pleased me. And so before leaving with my boots (more accurately, with someone else's boots), I gave the boot maker the money that I'd originally agreed to pay him.

Halfway down the road to my car, I remembered I'd left a bag at the boot maker's. Back in the shop, I caught him crawling on the floor looking for his keys. It was late in the day and he was preparing to go home. But he couldn't find his keys—not because they weren't in plain sight but because he didn't have the plain sight to see them.

The boot maker is blind or very close to it, and while I watched him on his hands and knees searching for his keys, I realized that he is too proud to stop making boots and the people in the area are too attached to him to have him stop making boots; so people come to his shop to order handmade boots, knowing full well that they will walk away in someone else's.

The horse races of Ronciglione run in front of the Casa del Mutilato, which is just down the street from the boot maker. Amputees who have picked up their checks at the Casa are likely to sit at the café on the ground floor and place bets on the races.

The horse races begin in front of the church at the edge of town. By the time the horses have reached the Casa, they have been running full out and slightly down-hill for more than a hundred yards. A narrow stone gate stands between the church and the Casa, and if not all of the horses that started the race pass the Casa, it is because they have broken their necks on the gate.

Those horses that make it to the Casa have another fifty yards before an intersection at which they must make a ninety-degree turn. It is here that the horses are most likely to flip over or slide into the side of a building, releas-ing their entrails in a great column of blood; and if the horses make it beyond this point, they must still ascend a steep hill of another hundred yards, where they are forced through yet another turn before the race is over.

Most horse races, even if run through the center of a

city, would be designed to avoid turns that would result in the death of the horses, and even if such turns were unavoidable, there would be jockeys to slow the horses. But the streets of Ronciglione were not designed for horse racing, and the horses of Ronciglione have no jockeys. In its riderless horse races, Ronciglione has created an event that combines the brutality of a bullfight and the wildness of a stampede.

Just a block from the final stretch of the race course is Ada Tacconelli's store. Now in her seventies, Ada is diminutive, sweet, and soft-spoken. She comes from a family of sisters who live and work in Ronciglione and who are all well liked.

Ada's shop is spotless. Not a drop of blood marks the floors or walls; there is not a whiff of decaying flesh. The instruments used to gut the animals are out of sight. Even when she is tearing meat from a carcass, she does it gently.

It is not only her demeanor and the tidiness of her shop that make her unique among the butchers of Ronciglione. For forty-three years Ada has quietly overseen the slaughter and display of only one type of meat—horse meat—and one and only one type of horse meat—meat from the marimano horse, a breed local to the region. Ada maintains that horse meat is leaner, more flavorful, and, owing to the absence of hormones, healthier than anything that one finds at the other butchers'.

Back in Sutri I stopped in on the owner of a local restaurant. He was known for preparing meat, and after some discussion of the many ways in which horse can be served, he gave me this recipe:

1. *Flatten thin slices of the raw horse on a cutting board.*

2. *Cover the meat with chopped celery, carrot, and sausage.*

3. *Roll the meat around the celery, carrot, and sausage.*

4. *Place the rolled meat in a pan filled with chopped tomatoes.*

5. *Put the pan on the stove and cook the rolled meat and tomatoes for one hour.*

6. *Add a fistful of kosher salt to a pot of boiling water and prepare a pot of* tortorelli *(a pasta local to Sutri).*

7. *When the pasta is ready, remove the tomato sauce from the pan and spread it over the pasta. Serve the pasta as a first course, and the horse meat as a second.*

I thanked the gentleman for his suggestion and walked back home looking forward to the meal that Sheila would prepare.

Sheila and Michele were in the kitchen. They had

become great friends. They were both artists and both exceptional cooks. Together, they gathered local recipes and spent days exploring the markets of Sutri and neighboring towns. I would come home in the evening to find them immersed in lively conversation on the distinctions between different varieties of lettuce, the ideal dressing for *puntarelle,* Salvatore's grappa versus the grappa sold at Nicolini, the local plant shop. I could not pretend to keep up with them.

Proudly I displayed the horse fillets. They immediately went to work. Assisting them, I was grasped by an unsettling thought. I had ridden since I was a child, and horses were the only animal for which I had an affinity. I could not eat one.

The problem was discussed and a solution reached: Sheila and Michele would dine on the meat, while I would enjoy a pasta made with a broth flavored with horse meat but containing no horse flesh.

Their recipe for the pasta begins by dicing and sautéing one clove of garlic and one medium-sized onion in two tablespoons of olive oil. The sautéing should continue until the onion is translucent. At this point, place one carrot, one stalk of celery, and parsley—all chopped— into the pan and cook until soft. Add two marrow bones, one-half pound of tendons, one-half pound of nerves, one pound of horse meat, and a sprig of thyme. The contents of the pan are braised until the meat is brown. Salt and pepper to taste. When braising is complete, the contents of the pot are covered with water and brought to a boil. As soon as the boiling begins, reduce to a simmer. The meat should be cooked until it is extremely tender—no less than five hours. The cooking finished, the contents of the pot are strained and the broth returned to the stove.

Tortelloni is added to the broth, where it is cooked until it is done. Place the tortelloni and broth in individual bowls. Splash white wine over the tortelloni and add shaved Parmigiano. This last step can be done at the table.

For the more adventurous, horse meat is also served raw, as in horse meat tartar, or thinly sliced and marinated in lemon, salt, and garlic.

While I am told that the best horse meat comes from around Sutri, it should be noted that there is a strong tradition of eating horse in Sardinia: I have dined in restaurants in Tempio that serve horse meat and donkey, and for horse meat pizza, there is La Vecchia Costa, which serves *"pizza monticanaglia"*—topped with mozzarella, thin fillets of horse, and spices.

Over dinner, in the middle of a discussion on the merits of *agretti*, a local vegetable of unusual taste, Sheila mentioned how while shopping that afternoon, she had run into Dina and Gino, who offered to arrange the baptism of our daughter Nicolaïa, and to be her godparents.

It made sense. If there was a reason that the town, famously hostile to outsiders, had opened itself to us, it was because of the affection the Sutrini have for children.

Our daughter had a special fondness for the old men and women. She took her first steps in front of them and learned their names. She spoke Italian before English. She was in every way more able than I was.

To the Guidis, there was an additional link: Gino and Dina had a grandson, Federico, who was almost exactly Nicolaïa's age. The two liked each other and played together.

When I asked Sheila whether the baptism would be performed in the Guidis' house or the café, I was corrected: the baptism would take place at the Duomo, at a special time, and Don Erri would himself perform the christening.

This was more than I could possibly have hoped for. My enthusiasm must have been obvious, for Sheila had the expression on her face that emerges when she gets a full whiff of my stale personality.

"Your motive has nothing to do with the ceremony.

You want a good seat at the Guidi."

"None of which," I pointed out, "should interfere with what is in the religious interests of our child."

"And the fact that my parents are Orthodox Jews?"

I'd forgotten about that.

"You will recall," she continued, knowing full well that I did not recall, "that Jews do not believe in Original Sin."

If there was an answer to this, I didn't have it. On one hand, I was fond of her parents and would do nothing to upset them. On the same hand, she was right about my motive and ignorance. But there were also my morning trips to the Duomo with Nicolaïa, my experience with the fig, the gradual emergence in me of what felt like a soul—all of which would make the baptism of my daughter appropriate. I needed time.

"Perhaps we should discuss this later."

Sheila agreed. The good mood induced by Michele and the meal had evidently affected her.

The next day I skipped coffee at the Guidi to spend the day in the library. The library in Sutri is two small rooms at the top of a building that was once a hospital where lepers were treated. Across the street from the library is a chapel, its patron saint Rocco, the protector of lepers.

I felt a strong sense of purpose as I climbed the stairs to the library: a week of research on baptism would produce an argument so convincing that Sheila and her parents would have no choice but to hand our daughter over to Don Erri and the Guidis.

Collecting the books that I needed, I took a seat at one of the two tables set up for readers. The tables were no more than a foot and a half off the ground and the chairs just a foot across. I imagined the leprous men and women, missing bits and pieces of their lower torsos, including (if the width of the chairs was any indication) parts of their rumps, reading books in which authors attempted to conjure suffering that was not a fragment of what their readers were enduring.

I heard a noise behind me. A child sat down at the other table. Another child joined him. And then a third. I was soon surrounded by a roomful of schoolchildren. And their teacher. Having no other option, I remained at my table, a ridiculous sight.

Genesis gives this description of Original Sin: God, having created Adam and Eve, warned them not to eat from the Tree of the Knowledge of Good and Evil. The serpent caused Eve to eat the fruit from the tree and she gave that same fruit to Adam.

Suddenly, Adam and Eve were ashamed of their nudity. They covered their nether hairs with leaves and hid behind a tree. God, who was in the Garden, shouted, "Where are you?" Adam responded, "We're over here and we ate from the tree." Adam blamed Eve, and Eve blamed the serpent. God cut the legs off the serpent (which before this resembled a camel) and tossed Adam and Eve out of Eden.

The sin of eating from the tree is the Original Sin, which, according to Aquinas, is passed down to subsequent generations through the seed of the male. Baptism cleanses man of this sin—the necessary first step to becoming a member of the community of Christ.

My research had converted my ignorance into confusion: Why had God told Adam and Eve not to eat from the Tree of the Knowledge of Good and Evil? And if Adam and Eve were the beings of superior intellect that I was convinced they were, wouldn't they have already possessed this knowledge? But assuming, for argument's sake, that they didn't know good from evil, weren't they then better off as a result of their disobedience—a question (as posed by Maimonides) that calls into question the effectiveness of God's "punishment."

There was also the disturbing news that some commentators believed that Adam was originally a hermaphrodite—an obese fusion of man and woman.

> "Male and female created He them and
> called their name Adam." (Gen. 5:2)

The Original Hermaphrodite also appears in Aristophanes, who described the earth as first inhabited by beings that were oval, had four arms, four legs, and two faces. They were smart and arrogant and one day decided to scale the heavens and slaughter the gods. Zeus discovered their plan and sliced them in half.

Adam and Eve were the metaphor, if not the prototype, for the unsettling density of humanity (the empty crowding) that has been a canker in my consciousness since I was a child. And now, sitting there, lapping over the sides of my chair, the children surrounding me, I was being shoved into the murderous Nothing.

Returning the books to the shelves, I left my classmates.

I headed up to the Guidi for a last grappa. With no argument to change Sheila's mind, I would be forced to refuse the Guidis' offer to baptize Nicolaïa, and the otherwise agreeable Guidis would turn against me. My days at the café were over.

If horses in Sutri are consumed, they are also worshiped.

On one of our first nights in Sutri, Sheila and I came across a gathering of people outside the Duomo: men and women from the town, nuns from the convent, boys and girls dressed in white gowns, and teenagers carrying musical instruments. I joined them and waited, not knowing what to expect.

As nine o'clock approached, the crowd began to form a line, beginning on the road leading up to the square and extending past the Duomo to the end of the square. First the nuns, then the old ladies, the marching band, a man holding a statue of the Madonna, and then the rest of the congregation, including myself. All the while, Don Erri walked nervously back and forth across the piazza, looking at his watch and then staring down the road.

At nine, the bells of the church began to ring, and Don Erri, not having located what he was looking for, threw his voice into song, which, having no doubt a fine origin in his belly, was required to travel so far before it got to his mouth that it arrived there exhausted.

Within minutes, there was a clattering from the east. The noise grew in volume until it was unmistakable that horses were racing up the hill. Relieved of his obligation to sing by the deafening noise of hooves, Don Erri turned his attention to prodding us forward in pursuit of the horses.

The riders slowed their horses as they reached the Piazza del Comune, allowing those of us on foot to catch up. When we arrived in the square, the horses led us at a walk through the eastern half of the town. Those who have apartments along the route put out baskets of flowers filled with pictures of the Madonna, Christ, and, of course, their favorite horse.

There were candles along the path and in the hands of the faithful. The candles gave off a light, which, when thickened by the weight of the surrounding darkness, flowed slowly from one end of the town to the other, merging people, icons, horses, and flowers into a serene stream.

The calm of the light pulled onlookers into the procession. Those who came just to watch were now marching.

The event was so moving that some—more devout than myself—began to show physical manifestations of their rapture. When people in the procession started to weave, lurch, and then fall to the ground, I knew that something unusual was happening; and then I, too—never before touched by such a thing—started swaying back and forth.

Soon I, like the others, was flat on the earth, staring up into the light. I tried to move my head, but the spirit of all that I had doubted in the past held it down, and my soul, which I had been looking for and which I assumed to be nonexistent or at least in a heavy sleep, began to stir. But this reverie and its seeming infiniteness was snapped by a curious aroma from behind my head. Those lying on the ground, including myself, had been upended by the excretion of the horses. As the procession passed over my body, Don Erri, who had started in back of me, was still upright, marching forward as his congregation was strewn before him; and as Don Erri walked, though certainly steeped in devotion, he glanced every few seconds downward.

It was at that moment that I knew that this man, unlike myself, was far too clever for the town.

Time Ravishes the Day

FOR months before the *Infiorata del Corpus Domini*, the men of Sutri gather thousands of flowers from the valleys, meadows, and hillsides around Sutri. The flowers are stored in great mounds in the storage rooms that are on the ground floor of every building in the town. Because the rooms are made of stone and have no windows, they are cool and dark, which preserves the form and color of the flowers.

Two or three weeks before the ceremony, women set up chairs on the street, just outside the entrances to the rooms. There the women begin the process of separating the petals from the stems of the flowers. The petals are placed in large wooden baskets, which are returned to the storage rooms at the end of the day.

A week before the festival, the streets of Sutri are closed as artists, supervised by members of the clergy, cover the streets with painted outlines of religious figures and symbols. In between the figures, the artists paint elaborate designs.

Two hours before the festival, the storage rooms are opened and the people of the town—divided into teams—fill the outlines on the street with flower petals.

Whereas the shapes of the religious figures and symbols are strictly traditional, the colors used in the figures are a choice of the collective. As some members of each team lay the petals, others debate the arrangement and selection of the colors. The entire process is supervised by old women who sit on patios overlooking the street. If a consensus cannot be reached about what petals should go where, the old women are consulted.

As the ritual nears completion, there is the inevitable problem of certain teams running out of petals. At this point, children are sent racing back and forth across town, baskets of petals on their heads, distributing the petals where needed.

If the wind were to blow or if it were to rain, the entire festival would be ruined. But on that day, the day that I observed the ceremony, the sun drove out the rain and the wind spent its time elsewhere.

Minutes before the bells signaled the beginning of the procession, the town, having finished its work, engulfed in the reflected light of millions of flower petals, stopped to admire its creation. And then the bells rang and the procession began.

The elders of the church led the procession, carrying large banners. The elders were followed by Don Erri and the local bishop, and after the bishop, little girls dressed as angels, white-robed boys, the fraternal orders of the church dressed in uniforms, and finally men carrying giant crosses and images of the Madonna.

The procession trampled every petal in the town. Every design was crushed, every religious figure kicked to death —the crosses, the saints, the images of Jesus and Mary.

Sitting in the square after the ceremony, my gaze found its way to the words inscribed at the top of the bell tower—*"rapit hora diem"* (time ravishes the day). But once a year the people of the town have their revenge on time, coaxing it into the town with the petals and then crushing them before time can have its way with them.

The large front doors of the Duomo, normally closed, are open for the *Infiorata del Corpus Domini*. Those carrying the banners at the front of the procession pass up the steps and across the seventeenth-century portico, through the open doors, and into the body of the Duomo. The rest of the procession follows.

Beneath the feet of the congregants and extending the length of the center aisle is a mosaic floor, which—despite the sculpture attributed to Bernini, the crypt containing Roman, Byzantine, and Lombard columns, the paintings of Eugenio Agneni, the Baroque murals—is the most remarkable part of the church.

My attention was first drawn to the floor by Sheila, who used it as an inspiration for her paintings. In her research on the floor, she discovered that the artisans who designed and laid it were part of an extended family known as the "Cosmati," though the term came to be applied to craftsmen who worked in the same aesthetic tradition but were unrelated to the family.

The Cosmati worked in and around Rome and Sutri; and as their popularity grew, the family ventured farther north (the mosaic on the tomb of Edward the Confessor in Canterbury is signed "Petrus Romanus Civis"—Pietro, a citizen of Rome). Certain churches in Rome (San

Clemente, San Saba), the cathedral in Salerno, and the church in Civita Castellana are the work of the Cosmati, but little note has been made of the Duomo in Sutri, and yet the floor of the Duomo may be the most beautiful of all. What is known of this floor is that it was created during the twelfth century by Nicolo and his son Jacobo, lineal descendants of Paolo, the first of the Cosmati.

Best viewed in the early morning, when the light falls unobstructed across the floor, the mosaic is revealed as a dense pattern of geometric forms cut from colored marble, stone, and glass; those forms in turn are filled with other forms (rectangles, hexagons, triangles, diamonds) of equally splendid, often complementary, more often contrasting, colors. Until the Cosmati, the floors of Italian churches were largely white marble; the Cosmati, influenced by Byzantine craftsmen working in Italy, introduced stained glass, gold leaf, colored marble, and paint to their floors.

The intertwining of forms and colors in the Cosmati floors causes the eye to shift between sections of the floor in search of a unifying pattern. Patterns do emerge but quickly dissolve and then re-emerge elsewhere till the viewer has become so immersed in the floor that all else disappears. This floor, the product of local craftsmen, does not fit into the church, it overtakes it—obscuring the murals and ceiling, the saints, the crosses, the images of Jesus and Mary.

Skinning Spinoza

THE horse meat dinner was such a success that I took to collecting recipes on how local cooks prepared the animal. One of the men in the square gave me the name of a chef who was said to be a great lover of horse.

The chef worked at a private club not far from Sutri, and I went out to see him. Contrary to what I'd been told, he showed little interest in horse. When I asked him whether he objected to eating horses, he said he had no objection at all; it was just not his favorite meat. When I asked what was, he shrugged.

Weeks later I ran into him at a bar. He was sitting at a table staring at the parking lot. He was distracted and fidgety. Perhaps in pain.

As he left, the owner of the bar and his wife exchanged glances.

I returned to the bar on different occasions and, late one evening, asked the owner about the man. The owner began to say something, but his wife cut him off. Whatever there was to know about the chef, I was not going to hear about it.

One afternoon, I was at the bar when the owner's wife was out. The owner knew what I wanted to ask, and I could see that he was debating with himself.

As he slid my drink across the bar, he whispered, "Spinoza."

There was only one possible explanation. The man whom I had bothered with my request for horse meat recipes was not only a chef but a thinker, and his dismissive response to my questions about food was his reproof of a life wasted on matters of no real significance. It would not have shocked me to find out that he had once been a member of the clergy.

"Spinoza" was the perfect name for him. I imagined I would spend days sitting in that bar, in discussion with him, receiving his instruction. Images of Sheila and Nicolaïa came to me: instead of spending my time searching for ways to cook horse, looking for the best boot maker, waiting for Aurellio Mezzadonna to come out of his palazzo, I should be back home—with my family.

That evening I had dinner with Sheila and Paolo at Sfera d'Oro. As soon as we sat down, I told them of my experience at the bar and of my insight and of my intention to call Spinoza and arrange to meet him. Just saying this gave me a sense of well-being. I leaned over and patted Nicolaïa's head.

During the dinner, under an ingenious pretext (a discussion of hiking in the Cimini Mountains), Paolo pointed out that the Italian word for porcupine, an animal found in the Cimini, was *istrice*, but the local slang was *spinosa*. With this, the truth of my experience at the bar popped up like a jack-in-the-box: the bartender had not whispered the name of a seventeenth-century Dutch philosopher but the local slang for a spiky animal.

The next day, I ran into Vittore and repeated the story of the chef. Upon the first mention of "*spinosa*," Vittore brought his finger to the side of his face, embedded it in his cheek and rotated it back and forth. Words were unnecessary—Vittore had provided the local gesture for something that is indescribably good. The mystery was solved: The chef was a porcupine eater.

Vittore and those with whom I spoke later believe the

porcupine indigenous to Sutri to be the most delicious of all meat in the region. These porcupine eaters admit to a sort of addiction.

I decided that I needed to eat a porcupine.

There was one obstacle: the Italian government had placed porcupine on the protected species list. Porcupine eaters were forced either to give it up or to continue hunting in secret, risking fine or imprisonment.

There was, however, a fellow named Sandro who claimed that he had discovered a means of hunting porcupine without violating the law. He would, if I was willing, take me on a hunt. As for how we would be hunting, he said nothing more than that we would be using his car. I assumed from this that we would drive to some remote part of the countryside and from there track the porcupine and shoot it.

The call came one evening. Sandro would be outside my house in just a few minutes.

As Sandro and I drove away from Sutri, I examined the inside of the car. There were no guns or bows, no knives or any other device for hunting. Instead, the car was full of books, scattered across the seats and floor of the car. When I asked where the guns were, Sandro responded that guns were unnecessary.

Approaching Lake Bracciano, we passed Roman ruins and the grave of a man from Sutri who was a translator of Ovid and who was famous for an inscription that was never placed on his tombstone. Well after his death, a letter was found among his papers requesting that his name not be placed on his tombstone and that instead the tombstone be engraved with a riddle:

> I who lie down in this place was a hunchback,
> Was from Sutri, and was a learned man.
> I was a friend of Nazoni.
> I say no more so as to ruin not the verse.

"Nazoni," according to Romolo, translates as "Big Nose," and was one of Ovid's nicknames. It is said that when the translator was asked his name, he would respond, "Anyone who knows Ovid, knows me." Romolo, himself learned and humble, is fond of repeating this story.

By the time we reached the other side of Lake Bracciano, all light had disappeared. Lake Bracciano is, like Lake Vico, formed from a volcano. The lake produces excellent fish, and a pope is said to have died after eating dozens of the lake's eels at one sitting.

After another half hour, Sandro slowed the car.

Reaching under the front seat, he pulled out a floodlight and trained it on the side of the road. His method was now clear: he was hoping to find a porcupine that had been hit by a car. A porcupine killed by accident, he asserted with the authority of a jurist, could be eaten without violating the law. It would be ideal, he added, to find one that was dying but not yet dead; that way, he could be certain that it was fresh.

The alternative was to go to an animal hospital and search for a porcupine that had been brought in for treatment but had passed away and been discarded. This was not, Sandro insisted, a manly way to hunt porcupine.

When an hour with the floodlight turned up nothing, he brought it back into the car and, still driving, switched off all the lights, including the headlights; by making the car invisible, he explained, he would create the "accident" that would kill the porcupine. This then is what he meant when he said, "We will use the car."

He evidently interpreted my silence as a questioning of his judgment on the legality of killing porcupines by driving a car around with the lights off, for he began searching the back of the car for a copy of the relevant statute.

At this point there was the very real possibility that he

would kill us before we killed a porcupine. When I suggested as much to him, he declared that he was "prepared to be eaten," by which he meant that having spent years tracking and consuming dead and near-dead porcupines, he was in no position to object if the porcupines—finding him bleeding and plump on the side of the road—decided to feast on his body. In some ways, he confessed to me, it would make him feel better.

Had he ever been in an accident?

"I once ran into another car."

"Another hunter?"

"Perhaps. His lights were off."

We brought back no porcupines that evening.

I am not sure how the chef had resolved the problem of being addicted to a species that could no longer be legally acquired. From the look of him that afternoon in the bar, he was suffering either the physical effect of porcupine withdrawal or the moral anguish of a belly full of it.

I had all but lost hope of eating a porcupine, when very late one evening I was approached by a man in the Piazza del Comune. Before he spoke, he pulled me to a corner where there was no risk of being overheard. There he informed me, without ever mentioning his name, that he had a *spinosa*.

This man was a dealer in black-market porcupines. He was hairless, round, and muscular—a bunion. If someone in town came across a porcupine on the road or had hunted one, they could sell it to him and he would store it until someone was willing to pay the large price he demanded.

I asked the porcupine dealer to give me some time. It was not only the cost that bothered me. It was also the fact that the animal wasn't skinned. The skinning of a porcupine, I was repeatedly warned, is by no means easy.

When I told one of the men in the piazza of my reservations, he laughed. There was a secret to skinning a porcupine, and if I just followed his instructions, the process would be as effortless as plucking a chicken.

The first step, according to my instructor, is to turn the porcupine upside down. Placing the porcupine in this position should expose bald patches on the bottom of its feet.

The skinner then steps back from the porcupine, places his hands on the sides of his body, and inhales as much air into his lungs as possible, holding the air in his lungs until there is no choice but to exhale. The skinner must repeat this exercise two or three times.

With this completed, a sharpened knife is held with both hands directly in front of the skinner's body. Approaching the porcupine with the knife held out, taking care to walk slowly and deliberately, the skinner shifts his concentration to one of the bald patches on the feet. As soon as the porcupine is within reach, the knife is plunged into the patch, making sure to create an incision of no more than four inches.

The incision done, the knife is set aside, and the skinner begins to fill his lungs. His lungs filled with as much air as possible, the skinner bends over the porcupine and wraps his lips around the hole. Making certain that his lips are tightly sealed on the porcupine (the blood from the hole should be spit out), the skinner's lungs are expelled into the interior of the animal.

Repeating this three or four times—inhaling and then releasing air into the hole—causes the skin and quills of the porcupine to drop off the meat. The rest is easy.

I was not wholly convinced that the method described by my instructor would succeed in removing the quills from the porcupine, but I knew that I was not about to try it. I'd done some skinning in the past, but it had never involved such an intimate acquaintance with the animal.

I would have to find someone who was capable of skinning and cooking a porcupine and who, at the same time, would not be bothered by being an accessory to the crime of consuming a member of an endangered species. There was no shortage of men or women in Sutri who satisfied these requirements. Perhaps the entire town. I picked Salvatore.

Salvatore's domain is Il Buco ("The Hole"), and it was at Salvatore's that I ate my first meal in Sutri, and it will be at Salvatore's that I eat my last.

Il Buco is located on one of the shortest, narrowest, and darkest streets in Sutri. True to its name and location, it is a hole dug out of the side of a building, as if the building had been operated on years before and the wound had not properly closed.

The dining room of Il Buco has no more than five tables, with the rest of the room taken up (in order of increasing size) by the refrigerator, Salvatore, and the fireplace. On the walls of Il Buco—originally white, now covered in a smoke-gray patina—are three small paintings, one of which is a portrait of a woman who appears to be gagging on a sausage. The painter was a woman who realized some notoriety during her lifetime, and who, Salvatore claims, dined at Il Buco.

Despite the great amounts of heat and smoke generated by the fireplace, Salvatore stands his ground, sliding meat in and out of the flames, his arms down the throat of the fire. The fire does not affect Salvatore. He is its master. Salvatore is Vulcan.

There is no one in the region who knows how to cook meat better than Salvatore. His offerings include beef, lamb, pig, wild boar, stuffed pigeon, sausage, and goat. If there is something more exotic that is not on the menu, with a day or two's notice, Salvatore will have it. Meat eaters come to Il Buco to eat, but also to worship Salvatore.

When he is not at his fireplace, Salvatore sits and stares at it, as if challenging it to come forth into the restaurant. Toward his customers, he shows nothing but indifference.

Most of Salvatore's customers sense this and leave Salvatore alone, and consequently Il Buco takes on the appearance of a Buddhist monastery—the master sitting silently as his disciples attempt to cause him as little trouble as possible. Even when his customers grow disruptive, Salvatore remains calm.

Disruption in Salvatore's restaurant is more often than not the result of Salvatore's wine, which comes from the unmarked containers Salvatore keeps in a cantina on the via Eugenio Agneni. It is regarded as the best wine in Sutri, and anyone who needs wine for their home simply shows up at Il Buco with an empty bottle or milk carton or even a glass and Salvatore fills it. Salvatore liberally dispenses his wine to the customers of Il Buco. After dinner, Salvatore pours a grappa of his own making that is as good, certainly as powerful, as any around.

On one of my first visits to Il Buco, two brothers came for dinner and as soon as they sat down, began arguing over a soccer match that they had just attended. Their disagreement spread to other matters and by the time the food was served, one of the brothers had called the other an idiot. The idiot responded that since they were both from the same mother, his brother must also be an idiot. To this, the brother said (and I paraphrase here), "From the same mother, but from a different orifice."

This accusation set off a round of shouting, which led to shoving, which led to the brothers grabbing their knives and lunging at each other from opposite sides of the table. While his customers fled, Salvatore sat quietly. Perhaps it was the sight of the undisturbed Salvatore that led the brothers to interrupt their quarrel before they speared each other. Returning to their seats, they drank a couple of bottles of Salvatore's wine and by the end of the meal were bleating with affection. I think Salvatore would have preferred if they'd killed each other.

All of this might suggest that Il Buco would be an extremely unpleasant atmosphere in which to have a very pleasant meal. That would be so, but for one rather remarkable fact: Salvatore, a massive man with a rough complexion, has a daughter of rare beauty. She transforms the place into something lovely. Men and women come to admire her.

What is ultimately most remarkable about Salvatore is that everyone in Sutri believes that beneath his gruff, laconic exterior is a friendly and sensitive man—and of this, I have no doubt. Luciano, a man who is fond of no one, adores Salvatore. "Salvatore seems tough," Luciano says, "but you can slice him with a fork." So powerful is this feeling about Salvatore that he may be the best-liked person in Sutri.

Needing Salvatore to help me with the porcupine, I walked down the alley to Il Buco but found the door locked. Sheila told me that someone from *La Repubblica*, one of Italy's largest papers, had found his way to Il Buco and written a review worthy of one of Italy's best restaurants. As soon as it came out there were lines outside of the restaurant—mostly Romans who had driven up to

Sutri to try the new discovery. Salvatore, unable to get rid
of the customers he already had, found the prospect of
more people crowding his restaurant so irritating that he
closed Il Buco and took his family to Naples.

When Salvatore returned from Naples, but before he
reopened Il Buco, I met him at the Guidi. In the café that
night were Michele, Paolo, and Enrico.

Since Sheila informed the Guidis that Nicolaïa would
not be baptized, I'd avoided the café. As Gino Guidi
approached the table, I anticipated the various means of
punishment that he might deploy.

Standing over me, his white apron gleaming like armor
from the light of the moon, he raised his fist. I readied for
the blow.

But I felt nothing.

Gino's fist opened. A glass.

"Drink."

Grappa.

The Guidis had not taken offense at our failure to
accept their offer to be the godparents of our child. More
impressively, they had not been insulted by my assumption
that they would take offense. That assumption was my sin,
and I was being offered the clear liquid of their forgive-
ness. It was I who needed baptism, not Nicolaïa.

From the beginning of my conversation about the porcupine, it was evident that Salvatore, though willing to prepare it, was not fond of the animal. This led Enrico to offer to slaughter a male goat and have Salvatore roast it. Salvatore said no, not because he disliked goat but because he disliked male goat. What followed was a debate between Enrico and Salvatore on the taste of male versus female goat.

The intensity of the debate was encouraged by Enzo Guidi, Gino's brother, who arrived at the table with a tray of *Etrusco*, a drink created by Enzo himself. After the *Etrusco*, Enrico put forward a series of technical and well-considered explanations of why male animals generally taste better than females. Each argument was met by a grunt from Salvatore, who, when Enrico was finished, gave a brief and unrepeatable retort along the lines of "You like girls; why should it be different with goats."

In the middle of the debate, Salvatore announced that he had just purchased two lambs—one male and one female—and that if he prepared both, it would be clear to us that the female was more delicious.

"You purchased the two lambs to mate?" Michele inquired.

"I don't mate with animals," replied Salvatore, followed

by a roar of such sustained laughter from Salvatore that he nearly dropped off his chair.

When Salvatore finally stopped laughing, he told us that he had once laughed so hard that he passed out and when he woke he had forgotten what he had been laughing about. This story prompted Enzo to remark that there were people who actually died laughing, which Michele followed with the observation that it was really not such a bad way to go.

Salvatore, who could not have been in a better mood, turned suddenly sour and rose from the table.

"Death by laughing is the death of a fool!"

With that, Salvatore left the Guidi.

In the end, I rejected the black-market porcupine—it was frozen, and Salvatore had no interest in cooking it. Instead, Salvatore hosted a dinner for twenty at Il Buco featuring a female lamb that was without question exceptional.

Salvatore might one day die laughing, but he will not die a fool.

Astrid's Story

SHEILA and I had been in Sutri for no more than a
month when Astrid called. She was in Rome and
wanted to see us. There was a tone in her voice
that I'd not heard before. Within an hour, she was at the
Guidi.

Astrid was a painter from Sweden. Her appearance was
comely, her mood sunny, but her spirit brackish, a jumble
that produced an exquisite neutrality. Other people were
of no concern to her, but she was always generous; men
and women found her sexually attractive, but she was
indifferent to both; having spent years attempting to
understand herself, she found little of interest.

As soon as she sat down in the piazza, she began her
story. The story concerned a man—an American.

She had met him at the opening of one of her shows in Stockholm. In Sweden on business, he had walked by the gallery on his way to a meeting. The owner was hanging the show and invited the man to the reception.

That night the owner went out of his way to introduce him to those at the reception. Astrid spoke to him for only a few minutes before she was taken away to talk to others. When she returned, he was gone.

At the end of the reception a number of people asked the gallery owner about buying the work, but he told each of them the same thing: the show was sold out. What he did not tell them, because he had been instructed not to, was that the entire show had been purchased by the American.

At a dinner after the reception, the gallery owner let the artist know that the American had bought out the show. He may have thought she wouldn't care.

But she did care. There was something about the American that she liked. His looks—blond, young, and tanned—but also his self-confidence and his contempt for convention, which allowed him to wear a sweat suit to the opening, to speak unguardedly about her art, and even to chastise the gallery owner for selling the work at well over what it was worth. Even his odor was offensive.

He was supposed to come to the gallery the next afternoon to take care of the details of getting the paintings to America. She would stop by to thank him.

When she saw him, she knew she was right about him: if she was ever to be with a man, he was the one. He, it seemed, felt the same way.

The owner of the gallery made reservations for three at the nicest restaurant in Stockholm.

The American arrived that evening wearing the same sweat suit he had on the day before. He had not bathed. She would have been disappointed if he had done otherwise.

Over dinner his conversation demonstrated that in addition to being an extremely successful businessman, he had wide-ranging interests. Astrid liked the fact that he was knowledgeable about the arts and had traveled extensively.

At the end of the dinner, the gallery owner insisted on paying. The American was clearly embarrassed. He was not used to having others pay for him. He would like to reciprocate: He offered to take the gallery owner back to America on his private jet and put him up at his apartment. The gallery owner declined, but the invitation was open, and there was no doubt that the American was sincere in this.

After dinner, Astrid and the American walked around

Stockholm. To her amazement, he knew the city as if it was his own.

When he finally dropped her off, he explained that he could not stay in Stockholm much longer but he wanted her to promise him one thing. He wanted to meet her parents. She agreed, and that evening she called her mother (her father had passed away years before) and arranged for the three of them to have lunch in the small town just outside Stockholm where her mother was living.

Two days later she picked him up outside his hotel. It was a lovely day, and on the ride out, he entertained her with the story of how the car he had rented—a Bentley— had broken down in a busy intersection, and how he, with drivers honking and screaming, stood staring at the car. At the same time, he was late to a meeting at which he was essential. As it turned out, when he finally arrived at the meeting, the transaction had been concluded by his subordinates, and they had all gone out to lunch to celebrate. He had, in the end, not been necessary.

When she ventured that it was probably the last time he would have anything to do with a Bentley, he responded that, quite the opposite, he had purchased the car and was arranging to have it shipped back to the States. He was not through with it. It had taught him something valuable.

In the country, Astrid's mother showed the American around the house and grounds. When they sat down for coffee after the tour, he asked Astrid's mother what she wanted for the house. Nothing, she said—Astrid had warned her that the American would attempt to buy her something.

The American apologized. Astrid's mother had misunderstood him. He was not offering her a present—he was offering to buy the house.

Astrid's mother got up from the table and without a word to Astrid walked away.

Astrid went after her.

Astrid's mother was upstairs.

Astrid pleaded with her to give the American another chance. Astrid's mother relented, agreeing to have dinner with them that evening.

Astrid returned downstairs to the American. Thinking it best that she get him out of the house, they went for a drive.

In the car, Astrid explained that he would have to apologize to her mother. As she said this, she recognized that this was the very behavior that had attracted her to him—unlike other Europeans, who derided Americans but secretly envied their rudeness, she freely admitted to her fondness for it, admitted that she wished she could be like him.

The American assured her that he had no intention of throwing her mother out of her home—he had been caught up in the beauty of the house and in its association with Astrid, and he wanted to make certain that it never left the family. He could accomplish this only by buying the house and marrying Astrid.

And in this way the American proposed to Astrid, and in this way Astrid accepted. They would make the announcement over dinner.

On their way back to the house, the American spotted a house for sale. Stopping the car, he phoned the real estate agent. The American instructed the agent to have a lawyer prepare the papers necessary to complete the transaction. Everything needed to be ready before dinner.

The agent went to work, and within hours, the documents, a lawyer, the owners of the house, and a notary were assembled in the agent's office. The sale was concluded.

The dinner that evening was arranged at a local inn.

Astrid's mother invited a couple that lived in the same town; they were two of her closest friends; they were also Astrid's godparents. The two were well traveled, and he, having been an executive at a large company, knew a good number of people in New York.

Astrid invited her sister and her sister's boyfriend.

Astrid wanted her sister to be there when the engagement was announced.

The American was seated next to Astrid's godfather. So well did the two get on that Astrid's godfather proposed that he come out of retirement to work with the American.

Astrid's sister joked that the American was too good to be true and that Astrid had actually hired someone to pretend to be a rich American. This set off a game in which the Swedes attempted to stump the American with questions about New York: The Swedes would confer in Swedish and then present the question to the American. The game provided good amusement and the Swedes had the opportunity to prove how well they knew America. As for the American, he didn't miss an answer.

The dinner went on for hours. The American instructed the owner of the inn, who was a friend of Astrid's mother, to open his most expensive wine and continue pouring it. When the owner emptied his last bottle, the American stood, glass in hand, to announce that he and Astrid were to be married.

Tears filled the eyes of Astrid's sister, and even Astrid's mother seemed pleased. There were rounds of toasts, and a picture was taken of the group. This time there was no question of who would take care of the bill. The American had given the owner of the restaurant a blank check before the dinner had begun.

The next day, the American returned to the States. He would be there for just a day before leaving for Brazil on business.

Astrid stayed in Stockholm to make plans for the wedding. Though the American wanted the wedding to take place as soon as possible, Astrid had a large number of friends and family in Europe and the United States. The arrangements would not be easy, and she wanted to help her mother.

Every day that he was in Brazil, he called her. Their calls lasted for hours.

After a week in Stockholm, she was confident that whatever remained to be done for the wedding could be left to her mother and sister. She made her plans to return to the United States.

But her departure was delayed.

The check that the American had given to the owner of the inn was no good. Believing the problem with the check to have been an honest mistake, and not wanting to embarrass Astrid, the owner called the hotel in Stockholm where the American had stayed, hoping to get a number where the American could be reached. But the hotel had no record of the American.

The owner of the inn called the police.

The American, according to the police, was not an American. He was a Swede—a Swede who lived in the parks of Stockholm and who pretended to be a wealthy American. His English, his knowledge of America, his mannerisms, came entirely from American films that were shown at a movie theater near the park where he slept.

Over the course of a decade, he had spliced himself together and in doing so created an assemblage irresistible to savvy men, cautious women, and even the Swedish government, all of whom he had easily defrauded. Whatever he managed to steal, he spent on restaurants, wines, and other indulgences, but never on a place to live, as if this, too, he had learned from the films.

The owner of the inn called Astrid's mother, and she called Astrid. Everything fit: The American had paid for nothing, had met Astrid outside (not inside) the hotel, never had a Bentley, never paid for the paintings at the gallery, and knew the answers to all the questions about America because the questions and their answers had been discussed in Swedish before the questions were translated (needlessly, it turned out) into English. The calls Astrid received from Brazil were made from a public phone in downtown Stockholm.

When Astrid told us this story, her involvement with the American had not ended. The police believed that he was still in Sweden and that they would arrest him shortly. Astrid would be a key witness at the trial: because the picture that was taken at the inn was the only photograph that the police had of him, Astrid would be required to identify the photograph in court.

To be in love with a man—finally to be in love—and have this happen could cause enormous suffering. I said this to Astrid. I told her that she did not have to be embarrassed, told her that to comfort her.

But what troubled Astrid was not this—it was her realization that this man was no different from herself, the gallery owner, the executive, her sister, and all the others on whom he preyed: They were all pretending to be Americans. She and her friends had the money to go to America to pick up their disguises; he could afford only a ticket to the movie theater.

She refused to cooperate with the police and left Stockholm. She also refused to return to America. She would travel for the next months, and when she was done traveling, if the American had not been arrested, she would do everything possible to find him. And when she did, she would help him. She was not through with him. She was certain that he had taught her something valuable.

The Guy and the Non-Guy

FROM the beginning, which is to say around 1000 B.C., Sutri has been divided into two sections: one at the top of the hill (the "town") and the other at the bottom (the "borough"). The borough is bordered on one side by the hill leading up to the town and on the other side by a second hill. Dug into this hill are an amphitheater, Etruscan tombs, and the Church of S. Maria del Parto (Our Lady of the Virgin Birth). At the top of the hill is the Villa Savorelli.

Running through the borough is the via Cassia, which has been an important trade route between Rome and north-central Italy from as early as 40 B.C. The via Cassia was responsible for the emergence of Sutri as one of the more prosperous towns in the region. In addition to merchants and soldiers, the via Cassia was used by pilgrims and soldiers passing in and out of Rome.

Until the fifteenth century, the borough was the most important part of Sutri. In 1358, it had six parishes, five monasteries, eight hospitals, and twelve inns. Notorial records show a flow of immigrants from Tuscany, Piedmont, and Lombardy, and from as far afield as France and Germany.

Because the borough was located at the bottom of the hill and outside the fortified wall that encompassed the town, the borough was vulnerable to attack. In 1433, following three decades of continuous assault by the enemies of the pope, the borough was conquered and set afire by Niccolò Fortebracci. The pope, to encourage the reconstruction of the borough, exempted the people of Sutri from all taxes for a period of five years. But the borough never recovered.

In addition to its vulnerability to attack, the borough was also affected by storms and flooding. In 1493 a flood destroyed thirty houses and three churches, and in 1654 a storm resulted in similar damage. At this point, the total population of Sutri, which in 1358 had reached 5,000, was down to 1,300.

But the ultimate calamity was caused neither by Nature nor by the enemies of the pope. In the mid–sixteenth century, Pope Paul III, who as a member of the Farnese family favored the development of towns such as Ronciglione and Caprarola, diverted the traffic on the via Cassia to the road running from Monterosi through Ronciglione to Viterbo—the Cassia Cimina. Having lost its privileged position along a major trade route, Sutri watched as more and more of its population moved to Ronciglione and elsewhere. The Cassia Cimina remained the standard route into Rome until after 1900, when the via Cassia was restored.

Today, little of the borough remains: three or four narrow stone houses, an abandoned church, a farmhouse, and the convent of S. Paolo, which has been empty for years. With the exception of the convent, these buildings sit directly on the via Cassia, the road leading into Rome.

The distance between the via Cassia and the hill containing the amphitheater and tombs is approximately one hundred yards. That space—a meadow for cows and horses—is known as "the Lawn."

A small number of people live and work in the stone houses bordering the Lawn. With unrestricted access to the Lawn and the Etruscan tombs and the amphitheater, it is one of the nicest places to live in Sutri. Because there are no stores or restaurants at the bottom of the hill, the people who live and work there are required to climb the steep hill leading up to the town to purchase supplies or eat in one of the trattorias.

Owing to their isolation and to the unusual setting in which they live, the people who inhabit this area have become a group unto themselves, a community of close friends, whom others in Sutri refer to as "the Lawn People." Though there are no restaurants on the Lawn, there are two cafés.

The more popular of these is just across from the mechanic where Alberto Mezzadonna lays hands on tractors. In addition to espresso, the café sells tickets for the bus to Rome. The café is owned by a man who is known as Dirty and who walks so slowly, though suffering from no evident malady, that it takes him several minutes to get from the bar of the café to the drawer where he keeps the bus tickets, a distance of just a few yards. Any resident of Sutri will warn that if going to Rome, "you should add an extra half hour for Dirty."

As one passes in and out of Sutri on the via Cassia, the

amphitheater and the Etruscan tombs are in full view. What is not obvious is the Church of S. Maria del Parto. If the controversy over the nature of the amphitheater (Roman versus Etruscan) and tombs (Etruscan versus Falician) were not enough, there is an equally interesting question regarding the origin of S. Maria del Parto.

Located at the end of the Etruscan tombs, S. Maria del Parto is dug into the side of the hill that rises above the Lawn. Other than a small door carved out of the rock and located halfway up the hill, the church is entirely invisible. While everyone agrees that the cave was dug in the first century, what is not clear is who exactly was worshiping there.

The Church and its loyalists claim that it was the early Christians, and there is no doubt that not long after its creation, the cave was appropriated by the Christians (faded frescoes refer to legends of the Archangel Michael and the vision on Mount Gargano). But the truth is that the people who dug the space into the hill were not likely praying to Christ, but to Mithras, the Persian god of light.

During the first century A.D., the cult of Mithras spread across Asia, Africa, and Europe. Rome itself came under the influence of Mithraism as Roman emperors endorsed it as an alternative to Christianity. But Mithraism was not limited to the rulers of the Roman Empire: Extant temples, reliefs, statues, and documents show that the followers of Mithras were found among all classes and spread throughout the empire. Mithraism was particularly popular among Roman soldiers.

Scholars classify Mithraism as a "mystery religion"— a category of religious cults that gained wide popularity contemporaneous with the rise of Christianity, the practices of which were kept secret from the public. In the Mithraic religion, it was necessary to pass through an initiation ritual of seven steps—mirroring the seven heavens through which the soul passed before coming to its final rest. Any male, regardless of race or class, could become a member of the cult.

All ceremonies and prayers were performed in hidden spaces, and the typical Mithraic temple—dug underground or partially underground—was rectangular in shape, with continuous benches of masonry running along the walls on both sides. The room was inclined upward toward the end opposite the door. The ceiling was painted to resemble the firmament. The church in Sutri follows this plan.

Owing to the secret nature of the religion, there is little information on the theology of Mithraism. What is known comes from an interpretation of a relief common to the temples.

The relief tells the following story: Mithras was born of a rock and appeared in mortal form—a miracle that was witnessed by shepherds, who presented Mithras with gifts. Chilled by the wind, Mithras clothed himself in fig leaves. After vanquishing monsters that inhabited the earth and entering into a pact with the sun, Mithras subdued and slew a bull. The blood of the bull created life on earth, and the soul of the bull ascended to heaven, where it assumed the role of protector of herds and flocks.

Having created life, Mithras defeated attempts by Ahriman, the god of darkness, to destroy it. Mithras was taken in the chariot of the sun god to the place of the immortals. Before ascending to heaven, Mithras had a last meal to honor his efforts.

The similarity of Mithraism to Christianity—the initiation rituals, the mortal form of the savior, the presence of shepherds at the birth, Mithras as a protector of mankind, the Last Supper, the ascendance of Mithras to the heavens—has been noted. So too the democratic nature of Mithraism and Christianity—both were open to all men regardless of race, class, or age.

But Mithraism diverged from Christianity in the secrecy

of its ceremonies (involving animal sacrifices, the pouring of libations, ablutions, sacred meals, and adoration of the planets) and in the elaborateness of its rites of initiation (binding the hands with the intestines of a fowl, bandaging the eyes, witnessing a simulated murder). The popularity of Mithraism has been attributed in part to the sense of mystical fraternity engendered by these secret ceremonies.

If the Sutrini resemble an ancient people, it is not the Romans nor the Etruscans nor even the Longobards— it is the followers of Mithras. The Sutrini are secretive, fraternal, and mystically attached to each other. Joining them is a long and complex process. Leaving them is unforgivable. The man who sells tickets to Rome is known as Dirty.

The most senior member of the Lawn People is Bebe.

Bebe came to Sutri as a tall and elegant young man. Knowing no one, he decided that he would go each day to the piazza for his morning coffee and sit in a place where everyone could see him. People would eventually introduce themselves. At that time, Bebe had a favorite vest made of a red checkered material. Bebe wore it every day so that there would be no question of people noticing him.

Bebe followed this ritual for months—sitting at a prominent table in the square, drinking his coffee, wearing his checkered vest—and yet no one stopped to introduce himself. Even the owner of the café appeared to have no interest in Bebe.

Months passed, and with the weather turning cold, Bebe knew that he would soon no longer be able to take his coffee in the square. Bebe had abandoned the hope of meeting anyone.

It was around this time that a man, whom Bebe had never seen before, walked out of one of the buildings on the piazza and proceeded toward the table where Bebe was sitting. As the man came closer, Bebe knew that the man was coming to greet him.

Just as Bebe rose to introduce himself, the man stopped. As Bebe stood, his hand outstretched, the man silently examined Bebe and then turned around and returned to the building from which he had come.

The next day, having finished his coffee, Bebe turned to get the check, and there, immediately behind him, was the man from the day before. As Bebe began to say something, the man backed off.

Over the next weeks the man repeatedly returned to Bebe's table, surveyed Bebe, and then retreated. As Bebe was getting used to this, the man stopped coming to the piazza.

Later, in the middle of winter, Bebe was passing through the square when he heard a commotion. Everyone in the square was staring at a man who was strutting back and forth across the piazza. Bebe had no trouble recognizing the man: it was the same fellow who had been inspecting Bebe months before.

Bebe continued on until it struck him that the man was wearing his red vest. The man must have broken into Bebe's house and stolen it. Then, crossing the piazza to confront the man, Bebe realized that he himself was wearing his vest.

The man had spent months memorizing the vest and then copying it by hand. His vest was stitch for stitch the same as Bebe's. The job complete, the man was now parading it in the piazza in front of everyone in the town and, of course, in front of the very man who was known for wearing it.

This was Bebe's introduction to Aurellio Mezzadonna.

Bebe says that though he was initially upset by the incident, he got over it quickly: Aurellio, having finished with

Bebe's vest, went on to manufacture homemade bows and arrows, which he kept in a quiver on his back, and would wing at people sitting in the piazza. For reasons unknown to Bebe, but undoubtedly having something to do with the vest, Bebe was immune from attack, so that while people in the square could not enjoy a coffee without being pelted by arrows, Bebe was left in peace.

If Bebe had settled matters with Aurellio Mezzadonna, he still had problems with the rest of the Sutrini. There was a bright, well-mannered fellow, Bebe recalls, who spent almost all of his time wandering around Sutri with his best friend. The two had meals together, shopped together, and when everyone else left the piazza in the evening, they remained behind to talk. They seemed to need no one else in the town.

Try as they might, no one in Sutri could see the companion. He was, to all but his friend, invisible. Consequently, people in the town came to refer to the fellow as "the guy" and his companion as "the non-guy." Even the guy came to refer to his companion as the non-guy.

One day in the square the guy introduced Bebe to the non-guy. When Bebe responded that he was having some trouble seeing the non-guy, the guy invited Bebe to his house, promising Bebe that when he came over, he would be able to see the "non-guy." Bebe was reluctant to accept the invitation, but the guy insisted.

Days later, Bebe arrived at the guy's house and knocked on the door. When the door opened, there was the guy. Swinging his arm around to the empty space at his side, the guy shouted out, "Eccolà, the non-guy!" Bebe spent the rest of the afternoon with the two of them.

No one has seen the guy or the non-guy for years. The owner of the shop where the guy bought his produce told me that the guy had left town suddenly with no word of why he was leaving or where he was going. When I asked the shopkeeper what he thought of the guy, the shop-keeper responded, "The guy's okay, but the non-guy's the funny one."

The Philosopher told me that he had heard stories of the guy and non-guy but knew that the guy never existed. When I expressed disappointment that I'd been taken in by Bebe, the Philosopher, in a moment of weakness, attempted to comfort me:

There is a rule of logic, he explained, which goes as follows: if *P* is an affirmative proposition and non-*P* its negative, the negative of non-*P* is the same as *P*. The application here was straightforward: if Bebe had made up the guy, then the non-guy became a non-non-guy and thus, by force of logic, came into existence.

Since arriving in Sutri I'd done little but attempt to find something in my character that I could build on; but I'd found nothing and was getting desperate. Faith, Nature, work—none of them had taken hold.

The Philosopher was offering me a way out. I didn't need to locate something affirmative; I could simply expand the nullity. I would make my mark as the fully evolved Non-Non-Guy.

The aspect of Sutri that Bebe found most irritating was that he could not pass down the street or shop in the markets without people in the town whispering behind his back. The people, he was assured, were saying nothing more than "There goes the American" or "The American was just in my shop" or "Why would an American be living in Sutri?" The gossip, the Sutrini told him, was innocuous—just the normal conversation that arises when someone from a different country comes to live in a small town. And Americans, it was pointed out, were a subject of interest since they were rarely seen in Sutri.

There was nothing wrong with this. It made sense. It would all make sense, that is, if Bebe were American. But Bebe was Italian on both sides of his family.

Stranger still (and there was no reason for the people of Sutri to know this), if there was one person in Sutri who would have had reason to hate Americans, it was Bebe.

During World War II, Bebe was living at home with his mother and grandfather in Cassino. In the middle of one afternoon, Bebe's grandfather came to the house and told Bebe and his mother to leave. They went out into the garden, and seconds later the house was hit by a bomb. As the intensity of the bombing increased, most of the town, including Bebe's relatives, moved to a monastery that was at the top of a hill just next to the town. The Allies would not, they thought, bomb a monastery.

Bebe's mother refused to go to the monastery. Her family had a small cabin in the countryside, within view of the monastery, and it was there that she took Bebe. From that house, Bebe, his mother, and his grandfather watched as the monastery was subjected to relentless bombing from the Allies, who believed that there were Germans inside. Bebe's aunts and uncles, all of his cousins, everyone they knew in the town, was killed. There were no Germans in the monastery.

So when the people of Sutri gave Bebe the nickname "the American," he was understandably upset.

Decades have passed since Bebe came that first day to

sit in the piazza. During that time, he has set up a successful business, and in his spare time, he has developed a
career as an artist.

In Rome, Bebe met an American named Nora, an
artist, and they married. Bebe and Nora made a home out
of one of the old stone houses along the via Cassia and
there raised a family. Bebe's daughter is grown and lives in
a house near her parents.

Over the years, Bebe has spent more and more time in
America.

Bebe and Nora, in addition to their place in Sutri, have
a house in New England, where they live for part of the
year. Everyone in the family, now including Bebe, speaks
English. Someone who didn't know Bebe might mistake
him for an American.

One day, not so long ago, Bebe discovered that the
Sutrini no longer referred to him as "the American." He
was now—Bebe knows not why—"Electric Beard."

If Bebe is the most senior member of the Lawn People,
the most junior is Chloe.

Her parents run an antiques shop on the via Cassia.
The family lives on the first floor of the stone house

next to the store. Just above Chloe and her parents are Bebe and Nora.

As a child, Chloe played in the tombs and in the amphitheater. In the meadow between her house and the amphitheater, she rode horses. For Chloe, ostracized by the other children in Sutri, these were the few comforts of her childhood. The reason for her exclusion was that neither of her parents was native to Sutri. Chloe does not, she pointed out to me, have a single friend from Sutri, despite having grown up there.

Another young woman from Sutri, Sandra, who like Chloe grew up in Sutri and whose parents are outsiders, echoes Chloe's sentiments, pointing out that the friends she had while growing up were from Ronciglione. Both young women describe their Sutrini peers as devoid of ambition. "Children are born dead in Sutri," observed Sandra.

Chloe has now left Sutri for London, where she studies archaeology. The focus of her studies is the Etruscans. She aspires to be the first person to translate the Etruscan language. Her proximity to the Etruscan tombs and her near-encyclopedic knowledge of the history of Etruria have given her strong views on whether the amphitheater is Roman or Etruscan ("Romans built, Etruscans dug; the amphitheater was dug into the hill, so it's Etruscan"), whether the S. Maria del Parto was originally a mithreum or a church ("A ram, a Mithraic icon, was discovered nearby; that means it's a mitreum"), and whether the Sutrini are the modern descendants of the Etruscans ("No friggin' way").

When I asked Chloe whether she would consider returning to Sutri, she admitted that though she would like to, she continues to be troubled by the exclusion of those whom the Sutrini consider to be outsiders and by what she describes as a general atmosphere of irrationality. One incident left a strong impression.

While traveling along the via Cassia one evening, a truck dropped its cargo onto the road. When the contents of the truck struck a metal guardrail, the noise carried into the town.

Rumor spread that Chloe's father had been killed in the accident. Sutrini began calling and offering their condolences.

Chloe's assurances that her father was still alive and had been nowhere near the accident made no impact. Chloe's father climbed the hill to the piazza for the sole purpose of defeating the rumors of his demise.

Despite his efforts, the townspeople continued to

deliver food and flowers to his wife and her daughter. When Chloe confronted one of the visitors with the observation that her father was standing next to her, was still alive, and that she was not grieving, the visitor responded, "That's nice, dear, but it doesn't really matter."

I had my last conversation with Chloe at the Illy café. We sat on the terrace. The automatic car wash, which is not enclosed, was spraying in all directions. The car wash is mobile, which is to say that the car remains stationary while the machine moves back and forth. On a summer's day the machine provides a sweet mist.

Across the road from the car wash are the tombs, amphitheater, and the Villa Savorelli. The Villa Savorelli—built at the beginning of the eighteenth century by the Muti-Papazzuri family but later taken over by Count Savorelli—sits on the hill above the Lawn and opposite the town. The grounds of the villa include formal gardens, a box-hedge labyrinth, and a park of oak trees.

Near the grounds of the villa sit a small church, S. Maria del Monte (the façade of which is in the style of Borromini), and the remains of a castle. The latter is known as the "Castle of Charlemagne," the story being that Charlemagne stayed in the castle on his way to be crowned Holy Roman Emperor. Since Charlemagne was crowned Holy Roman Emperor in A.D. 800 and the castle was not built until the thirteenth century, it is unlikely that he stayed there.

History may deny Charlemagne his bed at the castle or, for that matter, his week in front of the bean pot, but it is having a tougher time with the story that it was in Sutri that Charlemagne found his nephew, sister, and brother-in-law living in a cave. That story, told many times elsewhere, is that Charlemagne's sister, Bertha, secretly married Milone, a cousin of Charlemagne's. Driven out of France, the two wandered impoverished and on foot through Europe. Taken in by the peasants of Sutri, the two were set up in a cave and provided with food.

Years later, Charlemagne happened to be in Sutri on his way to Rome to be crowned Holy Roman Emperor. When a young man stole food from his caravan and fended off efforts to subdue him, Charlemagne, reminded of a dream, sent soldiers to a cave in the hills. There they found Bertha and Milone. Bertha announced that she was Charlemagne's sister and that the young man was Orlando, her son. Charlemagne forgave his sister, and Orlando (Roland in French) became the chief paladin of the emperor.

Just down from Orlando's cave is the amphitheater. Carved out of the hill, the amphitheater was built as an ellipse with three graduated balconies decorated with statues, columns, and niches. Small doors off the arena lead up to the balconies. The doors are in the "T" shape that was typical of the Etruscans. It was the Savorelli family that excavated the amphitheater.

The Villa Savorelli—now owned by the city—is not open to the public, owing to lack of funds to restore the interior.

Chloe explained that the reason the public is not allowed into the villa is that it is inhabited by a specter—a former resident—who is trapped on the second floor. That man, reported Chloe, wears a cape, carries a sword, and has a face of mist. All those who have seen him are able to identify a feature (she would not disclose it to me)—a shibboleth distinguishing those who have seen him from those who pretend to see him.

When I asked Chloe whether he was the only such person in the area, she told me of another: a girl who lives in Sutri but is frequently seen on the via Cassia, attempting to catch a ride to Rome. Those who have picked her up report that as soon as they pass out of the town (just beyond the entrance to the amphitheater), the girl disappears.

If Bebe is the most senior of the Lawn People, and Chloe the most junior, then the Sculptor is the most alienated.

I met the Sculptor at Bebe's. He is a strong and compact man who spends his days breaking rocks and bending metal. His hair was uncombed and his clothes covered with the dust of whatever he'd been shattering.

We spoke about a number of subjects, but the conversation kept returning to the United States. He wanted to move to New York. I asked him why he had not already moved to the States, anticipating the answer given by all the artists in and around Sutri: New York was too expensive and Sutri, in addition to its natural beauty, had enough artists to provide inspiration.

But this was not his answer. The Sculptor was actually ready to go. He had made his plans and had packed what he needed. It was just a matter of clearing up a few details with the Italian government, and then he would leave.

Bebe laughed. The Sculptor, Bebe said, would be a Lawn Person until well after Bebe was laid to rest.

The Sculptor had been born in Italy. In the 1930s the Fascists revoked his mother's citizenship because she was Jewish. Having a mother who was a noncitizen, the Sculptor automatically lost his citizenship. As soon as the war was over, the Sculptor requested that the Italian government restore his status as a citizen. The government refused.

The Sculptor has devoted five decades of his life to overturning the government's decision. On the day that the government declares him a citizen, he will leave for America.

Marcella's Cantina

WHEN the woman at the Guidi said that Aurellio Mezzadonna went into the basement every night to row on the High Seas, she did not use the word *basement;* she used the word *cantina.*

The simplest form of the cantina is a ground-level room that is used for storage. When the tomatoes are ripe, they are brought into the cantinas, where they are crushed, bottled, and stored. The cantinas are where the petals are stored for the flower ceremony. From the outside, a cantina might be mistaken for a garage.

In its most elaborate form, the cantina comprises a series of subterranean caves carved out of the underlying rock and connected to each other by steep ramps. Some extend for hundreds of yards underground. Historically, these were used to store great barrels of wine in the consistently cool temperatures provided by the rock. When the wine had matured, the barrels would be rolled up from below and placed in a room on the ground level, where they were either moved to another destination or emptied by friends and family of the owner.

One of the most beautiful cantinas is owned by Marcella, a young woman who inherited it from her father. Her father was known for the large, drunken affairs that he hosted in his cantina. Tables were set up in a room on the ground floor, and an adjacent room was available if more space was needed. After the barrels were brought up from the underground caves, anyone who was too drunk to walk home was rolled down into the caves, where they would sleep until morning.

Marcella now hosts her own dinner parties. They feature candelabra and fine wines. When it comes to drinking and enjoying herself she is every bit her father's child.

During one of Marcella's dinners, it occurred to me that not one of the guests was from the town. When I asked her about this, she confided that a guest, a dark-haired beauty with long legs and a constellation of freckles scattered across a russet complexion, was her lover. Because no one in the town knew, she could not risk inviting people from the town to her dinner parties.

As I came to know the two women, I grew impressed with the effort they made in maintaining the deception that they were not lovers. They created the story of being old friends who were sharing a farmhouse on the outskirts of town for financial reasons. They built a second bedroom and bathroom and made sure that it had the appearance of being lived in by one of the women. Linens were always on the bed, clothes and books scattered about, and an entire set of toiletries was kept in the bathroom.

The two women were rarely seen together. They circulated in the piazza separately, had different friends, never shopped together. Everything was thought of, and the deception was a complete success. The construction and maintenance of this subterfuge in such a small town was a great achievement, and one of which the two women were proud.

One morning I was sitting in the square when the young woman with freckles walked by to pick up a pack of cigarettes. Next to me on the bench was a man who is widely respected for his commitment to the Church. He is deaf in one ear, and there is some question as to how much his reason has been diminished by old age. Nonetheless, every morning his family brings him to the Duomo and then to the square. There he sits for the rest of the day, drifting in and out of sleep.

When the woman passed on her way out of the square, the old man muttered what sounded like "*lesbica.*" I turned and looked at him, but his face said nothing. Nor did anyone else on the bench react. He might have said "*lassativo*" (laxative), as he was facing the pharmacy, or possibly "*lecca lecca*" (lollipop), for there were children in the square, or even some unsettling combination of the two, but by the time I had decided to ask him to repeat his comment, he was asleep.

After the incident with the old man, I paid attention to what people in the square said when the young women passed, and it didn't take me long to determine that absolutely no one thought the women were anything but heterosexual; the young men in town did not miss a chance to comment on the appeal of the women, alluding to encounters they had enjoyed with one or the other or both.

Nonetheless, the coincidence of the young woman

being a lesbian and the old man's utterance continued to bother me. So the next time I saw the old man in the square I sat down with him. Leaning toward his good ear, I whispered *"lesbica,"* hoping that this would prompt him to elaborate on what he had said earlier.

From the look on his face, I knew something had gone terribly wrong: If he had once said *"lesbica"* or anything like it, he had long since forgotten. Now, sitting on that bench, he was convinced that I was either asking him to find me a lesbian or was under the impression that he was a lesbian.

"Don Erri" were his last words as he hobbled away.

Pasquale's Nose

EVERY Thursday morning an open market is set up in a parking lot. Women meet their friends in the Piazza del Comune before going to the market and return to the piazza after shopping.

One Thursday I entered the Guidi but found no one behind the bar. Following the noise of a television, I walked to the back of the café, where I found Dina Guidi and two other women; the three had just returned from the market and were watching black-and-white film clips of Mina.

In her day, Mina—"the tiger of Cremona"—was a singer and national sex symbol; but when her husband was killed in an auto accident, Mina disappeared.

Rumors about Mina continue to this day. They say she lives in Switzerland and that her legendary beauty has been destroyed by obesity. Her albums, which are released with some regularity, sell out immediately. Among the women of Sutri, she is an idol.

The women who take over the Piazza del Comune on Thursday are, like Mina, suspended in time. Entirely proper—in dress, demeanor, the way they speak to their children, the way they look at men—they ripple with sexuality.

A middle-aged woman in the square recalled the story of a beautiful singer in the 1950s who was approached by a drunk. The drunk yelled out, "I've half a mind to screw you."

The singer wagged her finger at him and replied, "If you do and I find out about it..." That is the spirit of these women.

The men of Sutri appreciate these women. But it is not the beautiful women who draw the most attention. Beautiful women require little imagination. The real challenge is to find the extraordinary in the woman whom others don't notice.

There is a man in the square who stares at one woman and only that woman. As hard as I've tried, I cannot tell what he sees in her. She is smaller than average, has thinning hair and a torso that is more boyish than that of most middle-aged Italian woman. Her posture is less than perfect, and she has large misshapen buttocks.

On a Sunday morning, I was in the piazza with Nicolaïa, when the woman walked by us on her way back from the Duomo. Her admirer was on the other side of the piazza and, true to his obsession, was staring at her. Not offensively, but noticeably.

The woman was almost through the square when I caught Nicolaïa smiling at her. And suddenly I saw what they saw: the deformed rear end. Divorced from its relationship to other parts of her body or how hers compared with the same part of other women—in other words, viewed as a pure form—her rear end was of great merit. There was also a pent-up exuberance about it.

"Piñata," my daughter whispered.

At the Thursday market is a man who is known to all the women in the town. His name is Orilidio but everyone knows him as Ovidio. What distinguishes Ovidio's stand from the others is not the quality of his vegetables but the method by which he sells them. While other venders price their goods by weight, with the price posted on small signs at the front of the stand, Ovidio's stand has no signs, no prices, and nothing that resembles a working scale. While other vendors carefully select the goods for the customer (merchants in Sutri are generally insulted if the customer handles the produce), Ovidio has no idea what his customers have chosen. At any given time, dozens of women stuff vegetables into their bags. Ovidio, oblivious to it all, wanders around singing.

Ovidio's prices are based on his judgment of the person buying the vegetables. Once the customer has filled her bag, she stands before Ovidio, a rotund man, his apron streaked with the juices of vegetables. Ovidio examines the customer, and if his mood is right, if the customer is sympathetic, is wearing the right clothes, has the right manner, if all of this is aligned, Ovidio will charge nothing or next to nothing for a month's worth of vegetables.

The problem with Ovidio's method is that women with exactly the same bags of produce, presenting those bags for payment at the same time, pay radically different amounts.

This generates such jealousy that old friends have stopped speaking to each other. "You think she's prettier than me? Well look at that mole on her left side—the side she's not showing you." This sort of thing.

None of this has any effect on Ovidio, who continues to sing during the fracas. Irate customers can either pay for the vegetables, leave the vegetables, or continue to insult the person next to them. Most pay—and then insult the person next to them.

Every Thursday a young woman comes to see Ovidio in the market. She buys great amounts, and when she is finished, she rests in the Piazza del Comune, surrounded by her bags. From Ovidio, she invariably receives a good price, inciting the enmity of the other women in the market.

This woman's name is Sabina and she owns a restaurant (I Vitigni) on the outskirts of Capranica, a village just a couple of miles from Sutri. In Sutri, Sabina is the subject of remarkable rumors: the daughter of a butcher, she doesn't eat meat; she throws out customers who give the slightest offense; she is a conjurer who foresees the future by reading coffee grounds; and she, like Ovidio, raises or lowers her prices based on her sense of the customer. I could not resist a trip to Sabina's restaurant.

As I entered Sabina's for the first time, what caught my eye was not the minimal setting, the strong aromas, nor the unusually large number of diners for a restaurant located in such a small town; what drew my attention was that the customers of the restaurant had been abandoned, as the waiters, chef, and busboys crowded around to watch one woman eat her dinner. That woman paid no attention to the commotion around her. The woman was Sabina.

Until that moment Sabina had not eaten meat for three years. Not because she was a vegetarian, but because Sabina had not found a piece of meat worthy of putting into her mouth.

No one who knows Sabina would have accused her of posturing. Sabina, all agree, knows meat. Sabina's great-grandfather was a butcher; Sabina's grandfather was a butcher; so, too, Sabina's father; and now both of Sabina's brothers are butchers. Luciano and others claim that Sabina's brothers are the best butchers in the area.

That afternoon one of those brothers, Vittorio, had brought Sabina a piece of meat. The meat was from a herd of exactly four steers raised by a farmer near Cura di Vetalla. Vittorio knew the farmer and had made a point of being present at the birth of the calves. Every two or three months, he would drive out to visit them. On each visit he would insist on being alone in the field with the animals.

When Vittorio determined that the animals were ready, he killed and butchered them himself. He trusted no one else. He brought this meat to his sister.

As Sabina ate, her brother sat motionless at a table nearby, his head welded to his palms, the brim of his baseball cap pulled over his eyes so as to hide his reaction in the event his sister disliked the meat.

After two bites, Sabina put down her fork and, finding one of the waiters at the edge of the crowd, shouted, "Why are you standing there? Do you think something so magnificent should be eaten without a fine bottle of wine?" Cheers and congratulations, and off the waiter went to retrieve a bottle of wine, actually bottles of wine, which were poured well into the night.

There is no menu at Sabina's. As she approaches her customers, Sabrina announces the selections that she is willing to cook for that table. Baffled customers listen to selections that bear no resemblance to what they had heard Sabina recite to a neighboring table. If Sabina thinks that a guest's health requires that he cut back on certain foods, those foods will not be offered. If Sabina thinks a customer is simply incapable of appreciating a certain dish, that too will be unavailable. Customers whom she dislikes are offered little or nothing.

What Sabina serves changes based on what she finds

in the market that day. She does all the shopping herself and will serve nothing that is not local and in season. A vegetable or cheese that stands out becomes the focus of that evening's menu.

That night, Sabina offered as a first course a choice of four dishes: a soup with beans from Sutri and farro; penne with truffles, ricotta, and zucchini; penne with gorgonzola and radicchio; and fettuccine with wild mushrooms and truffles. I chose the fettuccine.

The dish is made as follows: Heat one-quarter cup of olive oil; when the olive oil is hot, crush a clove of peeled garlic and add it to the oil; add one whole hot pepper and stir-fry for one minute; discard the garlic and pepper; add six sliced, fresh porcini to the oil; cook three minutes and add salt; fold the cooked fettuccine into the mushrooms; add fresh truffles to the pasta; and serve immediately.

The key to Sabina's pastas is simple: anything that would be good on bread as a sandwich will be good in a pasta sauce. In most dishes Sabina uses very little oil in the cooking process but pours it raw over the pasta just before the dish is served.

For the main course that evening, there was only one choice—her brother's steak. It was the finest piece of meat I'd eaten. The steaks of Nebraska, the steaks of New

York, were laughable by comparison. The flavor of this meat splashed across the inside of my mouth with the first bite and remained there, strong and pleasant, for hours. Along with the meat came sautéed zucchini with black olives and burnt capers, sliced and pan-fried potatoes, sautéed chicory, and fried artichokes.

As I was finishing the meat, Sabina and Vittorio came over. Still too nervous to eat, Vittorio was drinking grappa, a bottle of which he placed in the middle of the table. Sabina serves superb grappas; she does not serve Grappa L'Aiola, the preference of Sabina's brother. He keeps a bottle of it, with his name written prominently across the label, behind the bar.

I had not finished my first glass of grappa when a very large and very dark man entered the front door. He had an enormous snout and a thick mane of waist-length hair. Searching the room, he caught sight of Sabina and began a terrifying rant, made all the more threatening by the Calabrian dialect that made him incomprehensible.

He charged Sabina.

Customers moved away from their chairs, as brave waiters threw themselves in front of him. The beast was faster and stronger than the waiters, and those that were unlucky enough to encounter him were easily tossed aside. All the while he continued to scream.

By the time he arrived at the table, Vittorio, the last line of defense, was ready for him. He held out a glass of the Grappa L'Aiola. The beast drank. That did it. Pasquale was pacified.

To say that Pasquale was pacified does not mean that Pasquale was quiet—Pasquale speaks without ever stopping. When calm, Pasquale simply speaks in a softer voice.

"Pasquale's problem," Vittorio explained, "was that we brought out the grappa without telling him. He had to hear about it from someone in the town." This was insulting, since Pasquale was Sabina's boyfriend, and Vittorio—Pasquale hoped—his future brother-in-law.

The commotion over, dessert was in order. The trouble was that Sabina refuses to serve desserts.

Why? I asked.

"I hate them, so why should I serve them?"

The customers?

"Let them go to another restaurant."

It is not exactly correct to say that she doesn't serve desserts. She will, given the right incentive, make them. The trick is not to ask for dessert, but to mention that you just returned from Rome and cannot imagine anything better than the *millefoglie* at Agatha e Romeo or the *zabaione* at Ristorante del Cambio, and Sabina might well take up the challenge and produce—not at that meal or even the next, but at some future meal and unannounced — a splendid flan or apple cake or even a *panna cotta*.

As a result of the grappa, the conversation turned, as it did every evening, to an ongoing dispute between Vittorio and Pasquale.

The source of the conflict was that Pasquale, a car enthusiast (though that certainly understates it), had become concerned that Vittorio was mistreating his vehicle, and Pasquale took it upon himself to steal it. Sabina lived in a converted barn, and it was there, in the living room, that Pasquale decided to hold the car hostage.

Pasquale drew up a list of demands that Vittorio would have to agree to before the car would be released. Vittorio, on the other hand, refused to discuss the demands until Pasquale returned the car. Sabina, far too smart to be drawn into a fight between her boyfriend and her brother, remained quiet, though she did let slip that having a car in her living room was a bit of an inconvenience.

This was not the first car that Pasquale had rescued. Pasquale was running a halfway lot for abused and neglected cars out of Sabina's backyard. In addition to the cars he had taken from others, Pasquale had a collection of his own, many of which he had restored and all of which he maintained with daily polishings.

In the course of his imbroglio with Vittorio, Pasquale invited me to join him for a drive in his favorite vehicle— a thirty-year-old jeep built for the Italian military. The jeep was constructed so that it could be stripped down to the steering column, floorboards, and wheels. But its most remarkable feature was that it could be driven, owing to its weight and a specially designed engine, under water.

I would have agreed to a ride in Pasquale's jeep had Vittorio not taken me aside to speak to me on the subject. "If your life is important to you, don't do it," Vittorio warned. "If you must do it, then make sure he sniffs your feet."

Everyone in Sutri and Capranica knows that Pasquale suffers from extreme and often painful reactions to the odor of feet. Certain feet cause Pasquale uncontrollable itching, others chest pains, still others lead to involuntary fits of laughter. One could tell who had been through the square by what state Pasquale was in as he sat at his café table. I once caught him with a pleasant expression on his face: "Chinese men," he confided, "their feet are the sweetest."

In a confined space, such as a car, the concentration of odors exacerbates the symptoms. Vittorio was worried that on my drive with Pasquale, my feet might cause Pasquale to fall asleep.

It is Pasquale's claim that his sensitivity to odors is the result of his unusually large nose. Vittorio disagrees, believing that it is not the size of his nose but the disproportionate amount of his nose that is taken up by his nostrils. Though it is not clear who is right on this, there is no doubt that Pasquale has an unusual amount of nostril in his nose. It would even be fair to say that if his nostrils were subtracted from the definition of Pasquale's nose, it would really be quite small.

Our discussion about Pasquale's nose was cut short by Sabina, who arrived with a tray of Turkish coffees and observed that Pasquale would not be driving anyone, as his license was suspended because of a recent chase with the police. This was enough humiliation for Pasquale. He left the restaurant as noisily as he'd entered.

Many have asked Sabina about her relationship with Pasquale, to which she always responds, "Pasquale puts things in perspective."

When I had finished my coffee, Sabina had me turn the cup upside down and minutes later began to read the pattern made by the dried grounds on the inside of the cup.

Where had she learned this?

From her mother, who had learned it in Kenya.

Sabina's mother, Paola Venturini, is the daughter of Aldo Venturini, the producer of the film *Roma Città aperta* (Rome, the Open City). Aldo Venturini, at a time when Italy was recovering from the war and no one had the money to finance movies, found Roberto Rossellini and paid him to direct the movie. Venturini put all of his assets at stake to make the film.

Paola Venturini has lived abroad for the last couple of decades as an official with the Ministry of Foreign Affairs. She currently resides in Uganda. Because of her mother's work, Sabina was raised in Africa and Greece, which explains why Sabina is fluent in English, Greek, and Swahili.

It was her interest in the cooking of each of the places in which she was stationed that Sabina's mother passed on to her daughter. It is not uncommon for Sabina, in addition to her Italian menu, to prepare a *zighni* (an Ethiopian stew), *pastel cileno* (a dish of minced meat, spices, corn, olives, and cheese), lamb couscous, or even a tandoori chicken. This was the food she knew as a child. It was Italian cooking that she had to learn to appreciate.

With the dinner over, and the busboy resetting the tables for the next day's meals, I mentioned to Sabina that I would be back in a few days with a friend from Sutri. When I mentioned the friend's name—Marcella, the young lady who owned the cantina—the busboy raised his head. "The lesbian—what a beauty."

There was no doubt as to what the busboy had said—and now no doubt as to what the old man had said; the old man was not talking about laxatives or lollipops, he was talking about lesbians.

I asked Sabina who else knew.

She was startled.

"Who knows? Who doesn't know? Everyone knows she's a lesbian—her family, Don Erri, everyone."

The beautiful lesbians, who had minutes before seemed so clever in avoiding detection, were the object of other people's cruelty and now my pity; the very people of the town, those whom the women respected and worked so hard not to offend, had subjected the women to a detestable charade.

One of the hazards of drinking too much at Sabina's is that the stairs leading from the restaurant to the parking lot are steep, narrow, and poorly lit. Forewarned, I was prepared for the descent.

What I was not prepared for was the hand that grabbed my shoulder as I opened the door of the car.

"Don't say a word."

The arm pointed to a car parked next to mine.

"Get in."

Soon Pasquale was driving me out of the parking lot, out of Capranica, heading toward the Cimini Mountains and Lake Vico. The roads taken by Pasquale were, he assured me, impassable by the police. The darkness of Pasquale's skin and the absence of streetlights made Pasquale invisible.

"Pasquale, you've become invisible."

"You can call me Doberman."

"Doberman?"

"A nickname. I have sixteen of them. Turko, Rollo the Compressor, Gum . . . "

As we drove, Pasqaule explained the origins of each of his names; but it was Doberman that was clearly his favorite. According to Pasquale and confirmed by others, he was born with the ears of a dog—human on the bottom and in the center but with large, fleshy flaps at the top. One morning, after he and his friends had been out drinking, Pasquale woke up to find himself locked in a cage with a doberman. Pasquale knew the dog because it had attacked a friend of his a couple of days before and there was discussion in the town of putting the dog to sleep.

As Pasquale moved in the cage, the dog advanced toward him. Pasquale reached for his knife, but before he could get it out, the dog was above him, her teat dangling over his mouth. When I asked Pasquale whether he had actually suckled the dog, he declined to answer but mentioned that there were examples of this in Italy. A reference (I hoped) to the legend of Romulus and his brother.

At a certain point, Pasquale stopped talking, and the sounds of the animals that inhabit the woods around Lake Vico filled the car. So too the fragrance of the lake and its foliage. As we descended the Cimini Mountains, the car built up speed.

Then it occurred to me: Pasquale had no interest in the countryside, no intention of impressing me with the loveliness of the evening.

Pasquale's purpose was to demonstrate the versatility of his jeep by driving us to the bottom of Lake Vico. Our increasing velocity was Pasquale's attempt to get up enough speed to propel the car as deep into the lake as possible.

The fear of death by drowning seized me, but was quickly shoved aside by a far more awful thought: Pasquale had never sniffed my feet.

In the confusion outside Sabina's restaurant, I had

forgotten Vittorio's warning. The silence that had let the sounds of the animals into the car was the silence of a sleeping Pasquale.

Drowning in Lake Vico was a distant and nearly amusing reflection when compared with an imminent and disfiguring plunge off the side of a mountain. I struggled to wake Pasquale, having accepted the improbable conclusion that Pasquale was more dangerous asleep than awake.

Pasquale, as Sabina observed, had a way of putting things in perspective.

The Ping-Pong Table

TO pass through the piazza without greeting a friend, without nodding to a shopkeeper or waving to a relative, is an impossibility. So when she did this, the oddity of it was enough to make me ask about her. That I'd sat in the piazza for months on end and had never seen her made it even more curious.

The regulars at the Guidi told me that her name was Vera and that she was not originally from Sutri. Living on the edge of town, she had no friends, other than the hundreds of stray animals that she kept in her house. She rarely came to town, and when she did she would fight with the shopkeepers.

Every small town, it seems, has its Vera—the old person

who randomly berates others and who becomes the object of cruel humor. I had seen this in the Midwest and had no interest in revisiting it in Italy. I asked no more questions about Vera.

The next time I saw her, she was standing alone at a filling station on the via Cassia. I was having trouble with the automatic pump and was looking around for someone who might help.

Vera approached me. I was prepared for her: knowing no Italian, I could not possibly be offended at what she was about to shout.

"Do you speak English?"

She was smarter than I thought. I prepared myself.

"Well then," she said, "if you stand back a few steps, I'll take care of this for you."

Watching her as she filled my tank, I saw that she was beautifully turned out; her short silver hair was perfectly done, her nails manicured, and her blouse a soft, white fabric intricately embroidered. She must have sensed that I was examining her.

"There are two things I love about America: Americans and Orlon. When I need a new blouse, I fly to New York." She returned the hose to the pump.

A week later, Sheila and I drove to Vera's for tea.

Vera's house is less a house than a villa. It is surrounded

by large lawns, and on those lawns are cherry, fig, and pine trees.

Inside, the house is decorated simply: leather volumes of Shakespeare, German poetry, an antique tapestry that she inherited from her mother's family. On the mantel over the fireplace were a silver vase and picture frames. Obscured by these objects was a yellowed Ping-Pong ball.

I asked about the ball.

When Vera was growing up, her family lived in the fashionable Parioli section of Rome. During the summers, Vera's parents would take her to resorts outside the city. There, Vera, an athletic young woman, learned to play sports, including Ping-Pong.

One summer, she found herself in the finals of a Ping-Pong tournament. Her opponent was Mussolini's daughter. Vera asked her mother whether it was all right to win. "Beat the hell out of her," her mother advised.

Vera was not so sure. Mussolini's daughter had polio.

Sheila asked Vera about her parents. Both Vera's mother and father came from wealthy families. Her father, an Italian Catholic, was a handsome man and a voluptuary. Whatever he earned went to fine clothes, rare books, and wines. When he ran out of his own money, he spent his wife's.

Vera's mother was more conservative. An Egyptian

Jewess, she was from an old and well-educated family. The family made a point of sending their children to the finest schools in Cairo.

Vera's father was working in Cairo, and it was there that he met Vera's mother. After they married, Vera's mother moved to Rome, where Vera was raised.

She was, she confessed, a "very selfish child." She greatly enjoyed the pleasures that came with being part of Roman society. Even with the war, she and her friends enjoyed themselves.

Early one morning, as Vera came down for breakfast, she tripped over a man lying on the floor. She did not recognize the man and ran to her parents' room.

The man, she was told, was an American pilot.

Vera knew that if the Italians or Germans found out that her parents were hiding an American pilot, she and her parents would be shot. But before this, they would be tortured on the chance that they knew the names of other members of the underground.

Vera argued with her parents. They told her to return to her breakfast, and if she could avoid waking the pilot, they would appreciate it.

In the months that followed, her parents became bolder, often taking in five or more pilots at a time. The pilots would stay for a few days before they were moved on.

Reluctantly, Vera got to know the pilots. The pilots liked her. With two or three she developed attachments.

While this was going on, Vera's family made certain that the rest of their lives remained unchanged; they wanted to give no indication to the outside world that anything unusual was going on. Vera and her parents maintained their friendships and their way of life as it had been before.

Vera's father, for example, had a tailor by the name of Ciro Guliano. The best tailor in Rome, Guliano was also a hunchback. Vera's father, who had an affection for Guliano, wondered what Guliano saw as he worked day in and out in front of the mirror.

Guliano's reputation was such that he was employed by the finest men of Rome. When the Germans came to Rome, their generals and officers had their suits and uniforms made by Guliano. Waiting to be fitted for his suits, Vera's father would see Guliano in conversation with the Germans as he worked on their suits in one of the several fitting rooms that Guliano maintained in his workshop. Vera's father was never allowed close enough to overhear their conversations, but he could tell that Guliano felt more than comfortable with the Germans and that they shared confidences with their tailor.

When Guliano was done with the Germans, Vera's

father would take their place in the fitting rooms. This made Vera's father uncomfortable, but he knew it would give rise to suspicion if he, one of the tailor's best customers, abandoned Guliano.

With the Germans still in Rome, Vera's father heard a remarkable rumor. Guliano, according to the story, was hiding pilots. But that was not all: Guliano was hiding dozens of them at a time.

Vera's father did not believe it. He had seen Guliano with the Germans, and besides, Guliano was a tailor—his apartment was small and there was no place in his workshop to hide anyone.

Nonetheless, one day when Vera's father was standing with his back to the mirror and the tailor was behind him, Vera's father, possibly to have sport with someone whom he suspected of collaborating with the Germans, confronted the tailor with the rumor. Assuring the tailor that he had no reason to believe a word of the rumor, Vera's father just wanted Guliano to be aware of what people were saying.

Vera's father waited for the tailor's response, but none came. Finally, he turned his head, hoping to catch in the mirror the expression on Guliano's face. But there was no hunchback in the mirror. It was a young man. A straight-backed young man. And next to him another. And next to him another.

Just behind the mirrors—in the fitting rooms where the Germans shared their secrets with the tailor—were the pilots.

The tailor knew that Vera's father was part of the underground, and as he stood with his back to the mirror, the tailor—possibly having sport with a man who had allowed his confidence in an old friend to wane—had swung open the door to the mirror.

Vera's father no longer wondered about what the hunchback saw in the mirror.

Vera's parents continued to hide pilots until the evening when the superintendent of the building called up to say that German soldiers had entered the building.

The Germans were not coming for the pilots. They were there for Vera's mother. They were rounding up Jews in the neighborhood.

Vera's mother ran out of the apartment, but there was no place to go. The soldiers could be heard rushing up from below, and there was only one staircase.

There were two other apartments on the floor, but one

was the home of a countess who regularly entertained Germans, and the other, the apartment of a prostitute. The prostitute had been purposely snubbed by Vera's parents.

In desperation, Vera's mother rang the door of the prostitute.

Opening the door, the prostitute saw Vera's mother and heard the footsteps of the Germans. Without saying a word, she took the other woman's hand and pulled her inside. The German soldiers raced onto the floor just as the door closed. When they could not find Vera's mother in her own apartment, they searched the rest of the floor. Upon entering the prostitute's apartment, they found her on top of a customer, whose face was obscured. "Excuse me," the prostitute reprimanded them. "Some of us have to make a living." The customer was Vera's mother.

Vera's mother did not dare return to her family, and for the rest of the war she lived in the sewers and parks of Rome. She would occasionally call on the phone, but always pretended to be someone else.

As for Vera, when the officials at her elementary school heard that her mother was Jewish, they refused to let her back into the school. Vera was taught by her father. She remembers the Germans taking Jewish children, her friends, from their beds, still in their pajamas, and, with

Italian soldiers standing by, shooting the children in the street. The Germans made certain that Vera witnessed the murders.

From her apartment, Vera saw the last skirmishes between the Allies and Germans in Rome. Vera was one of the first to come forward with food and drink for the Americans as they marched through the city.

In the years after the war, some of the American pilots wrote to Vera and her family, thanking them for their help. Vera decided to visit the United States.

On the voyage over, she met a man. Good-looking and with an easy manner, he went out of his way to make certain that in America Vera spent time with no other men, including the pilots. Wealthy, he took Vera all over New York, and when she was to return to Italy, he accompanied her.

It was not long thereafter that the two were engaged. Vera's father warned her against the man. Her suitor, Vera's father told her, was nothing like the men they had taken in during the war.

Shortly before the wedding, Vera received a phone call. The newspapers that day reported the story of her fiancé's marriage to an opera star.

Vera moved from Rome to Sutri. She brought her Ping-Pong table with her, hoping that it would help her make friends.

Vera found no friends. Vera contended to me that the people of Sutri disliked her. She decided that she did not want anyone from Sutri inside her house. She threw out her Ping-Pong table.

Vera began to bring home stray and abused dogs and cats. She claims the Sutrini have no interest in dogs other than to guard livestock. Their dogs are tied day and night to posts in the field, and if the dogs happen to reproduce, their puppies are left to starve.

In addition to her dogs and cats, Vera tends to her fruit trees. Because the trees block the light, there is no grass, only flesh-colored dirt. Despite this, Vera makes certain that the blades on her mower are razor sharp as she rides back and forth across the land.

When she is not gathering fruit from her trees, when she is not feeding and cleaning the scores of dogs and cats that she has taken in, when she is alone, Vera reviews the details of how she would have liked to greet the German soldiers who came to her home more than fifty years before.

"I will begin by slicing their thighs; from there I will move to their bodies, faces, and then their eyes. Their testicles will be last—punctured many, many times—with sharp, hot needles." The torture, she assured me, will be administered in such a way as to inflict the greatest amount of pain over the longest period of time—a sort of reverse utilitarianism. Vera's experience with abused animals has taught her much about pain.

One afternoon at the Guidi, I asked Enrico about Vera's thoughts on the treatment of dogs and cats. Trained as a veterinarian, Enrico is a forthright and gentle man. He would be honest with me.

Enrico does not believe that the Sutrini intentionally abuse their animals. Though there are a large number of stray dogs and cats, a problem that the city should address, the population of strays is probably no greater than in other rural communities.

I had no reason to doubt Enrico's opinion that the Sutrini are little different from others in their treatment of animals.

There is a possible exception to this:

A friend, Wendy, lives in Sutri. While her children were growing up, she would walk them down to Lake Bracciano. She and her children would watch a group of nutria that played at the edge of the lake. Nutria are large, ratlike creatures.

On a visit to the lake, Wendy and the children became aware, as they trotted down the hill to the lake, that all the nutria were gone. A man, who also appeared to be looking for nutria, was standing at the edge of the lake, and Wendy asked him what had happened to them.

"We ate them."

Containing her disgust so as not further to alarm her children, Wendy asked what the nutria tasted like.

"Cat."

Sheila repeated this story to Romolo and his wife, Mary Angela, who explained to us that when food began to run out during the war, people in the region would supplement their diet with cat. The Sutrini gained a reputation for this and became known as "cat eaters." Some in the area have not lost their taste for the animal.

As I spoke with Enrico, the drink, combined with the heat from sitting outside at the Guidi, began to affect me. I searched the piazza for shade. There was none.

Then I saw it. A gowned figure in the brightness.

Aurellio Mezzadonna.

That day he looked more woman than man; and his silk gown glowed, as if on fire.

Beatrice.

When she appeared to Dante at the top of the mountain of Purgatory, "the colors of live flame played on her gown," and Dante wept when he saw her. And if this was right, if Mezzadonna was Beatrice, then Romolo was Virgil, the beans were the instruments of my purgation, Frank an incarnation of the Original Hermpahrodite; and Sutri was Eden.

A hand touched my shoulder. "I need to tell you something about her," Enrico whispered.

So it was not a hallucination. Enrico had seen Beatrice and probably had seen her before. He began to speak. I trembled.

"I have her Ping-Pong table."

"Beatrice's Ping-Pong table?"

He ignored me.

"It's been in my father's cantina for twenty years. We thought Vera might one day want to play again."

Poets of the Arm

N one of the last nights of summer, a group of us drove to Barbarano Romano. We had been invited to dinner at Salvo's. He said it would be just a couple of tables set up on the back porch, a sort of end-of-the-summer dinner for his friends.

When we approached Salvo's farm, everything was quiet.

As we rounded the house to the backyard, there appeared in front of us an illuminated patio and, as Salvo had said, just a couple of tables—two, to be exact—and at each of those tables were, as Salvo had said, some of his friends.

But it was not easy to find Salvo. It would have been

easier had the tables not been more than one hundred feet long and each so crowded with people that some had to leave before we could sit down. The number of people moving giant platters of food from the kitchen to the tables was alone enough to fill a good-sized dinner party.

After hours of eating and drinking, the noise of the guests having grown to a point at which it was impossible to hear, a man stood up on his seat and braced his legs against those on each side of him. With no attempt to quiet the crowd, he announced that he would begin by addressing the subject of seduction. With this, he began to chant, and as he chanted his arms moved.

The man stood and chanted in rhyming verse for over an hour. His poems touched on many themes and into each poem he brought the stories of the guests at the table. Some left their seats in embarrassment, others wept, most laughed.

By the time the man reached the end of his poems, a thin froth of cloud had settled on the night's horizon and from the cloud burst bouquets of lightning.

The afternoon after our dinner at Salvo's, I ran into the old man who had uttered the word *"lesbica."* He was sitting outside at the Guidi. I sat down with him and told him about the poet I'd heard the night before. The man in the piazza explained that such a performer is known as a *"poeta a braccio"* (poet of the arm) and that there was a tradition of these men in the area. When I asked whether there were such poets in Sutri, the old man responded, "It's something to which we all aspire."

The remark reminded me of how much I admired the people of the town. But there was one thing that troubled me, and I decided to ask him about it.

"You know that the two young women are lesbians."

He nodded.

"And yet you and the rest of the town allow them to waste their time pretending they are something else."

He looked at me with an expression that suggested that I had lived in Sutri long enough to know the answer:

"Sutri is a small town and we don't want them to leave. What else would they do?"

At this moment I stopped being concerned by the great questions of Sutri: whether the Sutrini are Etruscan, Roman, or Falician; the origins of the Mitreo and amphitheater; the birthplace of Pontius Pilate; and whether Frank is a man or woman. I ceased worrying about these things because I realized, sitting across from that man in the square, that despite its modern context

Sutri was still an archaic society—a population that had, over the course of thousands of years, forged a collective identity and story and had a mystical attachment to both.

This effort, this forging, requires the continuous transformation of reality—and as to transforming reality, there are none better than the Sutrini: they sprout the appendages of animals, become butterflies, build palazzos out of wine, befriend invisible beings, switch back and forth between sexes with no more than the power of suggestion, disappear when they pass beyond the town limits, and heal tractors with a wave of the hand.

These transformations, mutations, myths, whatever one may call them, have become so integral to Sutri— they are the points of collective attachment—that their reality has disappeared. The Sutrini believe that they are Etruscan, that their town is timeless, that their postman is an oracle, Bebe an American, the woman selling shoes is a man, and that Chloe's father is dead though he sits reading a newspaper in the square. It is no different from tribes whose members believe that they can be sleeping in their beds as individuals and at the same time flying above the village searching for its enemies—or that the air is clogged with the spirits of dead ancestors.

It is likely that the mystical quality of ancient Sutri was

carried into the modern world owing to the unusually long period in which Sutri was under the control of the Church. An extended diet of the Trinity, Resurrection, sacraments, and assorted mystical events anesthetized the Sutrini to more modern ways of thinking, making it possible to construct a story of the town that departs from the "history" that is in front of them.

Gradually, slyly, but irretrievably, the Sutrini have gathered me into this process: tales are being told of me, Sheila, and our child, and these have caused people to receive us in a certain way and that, in turn, affects the kind of people we become.

But most revealing is that none of this has caused me to turn away from the town: there is no sense of extinction—no compulsion to find within me the immutable substance that will withstand the attack. The reason, I suspect, is an awareness that, while Sutri was changing me, in a small but not indiscernible way, I was changing Sutri. And this feeling of participation in a larger story has been enlivening.

The transgression of Adam and Eve was not in learning the difference between good and evil but in treating the knowledge they received as something that was, literally, internal to them—a food that could be seized, devoured, and controlled by the individual. The result of their actions was appropriate: they became comically self-obsessed—concerned only with their nudity, they attempted to hide from animals and from their Creator.

The Lord's "Where are you" was not a question but a condemnation—a warning against the consequences of losing sight of that context which was so vital to defining who they were and would become. Adam and Eve, having already lost sight of Eden, were expelled from it. Their exile from Paradise was not a punishment; it was a formality.

If the story of Adam and Eve is clear to me, the story of Sutri is not. If I understand it at all, it is still only a fraction.

But of this I am certain: when someone from the hazelnut grove shouts, "Where are you," I will know the answer.